ROBERTO BURLE MARX: The Unnatural Art of the Garden

ROBERTO BURLE MARX

The Unnatural Art of the Garden

WILLIAM HOWARD ADAMS

The Museum of Modern Art, New York

Distributed by Harry N. Abrams, Inc., New York

Published on the occasion of the exhibition
Roberto Burle Marx: The Unnatural Art of the Garden
The Museum of Modern Art, New York
May 23–August 13, 1991

This exhibition is made possible by a generous grant from Banco Safra SA.

Additional support has been provided by
Mr. and Mrs. Gustavo Cisneros and
The International Council of The Museum of Modern Art.

Library of Congress Catalog Card Number 90-64454
ISBN 0-87070-197-5 (The Museum of Modern Art)
ISBN 0-8109-6096-6 (Harry N. Abrams, Inc.)
Printed in the United States of America

Produced by the Department of Publications of
The Museum of Modern Art, New York
Osa Brown, Director, Department of Publications

Edited by Jane Fluegel
Designed by Susanna Stieff
Production by Marc Sapir
Printed by Colorcraft Lithographers, Inc., New York
Bound by The Riverside Group, Rochester, New York

Published by The Museum of Modern Art
11 West 53 Street, New York, New York 10019

Distributed in the United States by Harry N. Abrams, Inc., New York. A Times Mirror Company

Distributed outside the United States by Thames and Hudson, London

Front cover: View of the Olivo Gomes House and Garden, São José dos Campos, São Paulo, 1990

Back cover: Burton Tremaine Residence: Project. Garden plan. Gouache on paper, 50 1/4 x 27 3/4 in. (127.7 x 70.5 cm). The Museum of Modern Art, New York. Gift of Mr. and Mrs. Burton Tremaine

Photograph Credits

The photographers and sources for the illustrations in this volume are listed alphabetically below. Reference illustrations in the text are cited by figure number. Illustrations in the Projects section are cited by plate number.

William Howard Adams: fig. 29; pl. 29. Courtesy William Howard Adams: fig. 26. *Art et Decoration*: fig. 6. Eugene Atget, courtesy William Howard Adams: fig. 25. Courtesy Avery Architectural and Fine Arts Library, Columbia University in the City of New York: figs. 9, 11. Courtesy Brazilian Ministry of External Relations: pl. 55. Courtesy Burle Marx e Companhia Limitada: fig. 28; pl.14. Marc Ferrez: figs. 7, 8, 12–14. Marcel Gautherot: figs. 19, 24; pls. 35, 53, 54. Courtesy General Research Division, The New York Public Library, Astor, Lenox and Tilden Foundations: fig. 10. Farrell Grehan: fig. 1; pls. 31, 33, 36, 46, 56–58. Ellen Grossman, courtesy Burle Marx e Companhia Limitada: pl. 18. Ellen Grossman, courtesy Conrad Hamerman: fig. 23; pls. 23, 27, 34, 40, 50, 51. Kate Keller: pls. 12, 13 and back cover, 52. Man Ray, copyright © 1991 ARS NY/ADAGP: fig. 5. Michael Moran: figs. 3, 4, 17, 21, 22 and front cover, 27; pls. 16, 19–22, 24–26, 28, 30, 32, 37, 38, 41–45, 47–49, 60–62. The Museum of Modern Art, New York: figs. 18, 20. Mali Olatunji, courtesy Burle Marx e Companhia Limitada: pl. 59. Haruyoshi Ono: fig. 2. Haruyoshi Ono, courtesy Burle Marx e Companhia Limitada: fig. 16; pls. 1–11. Courtesy Safra Group Headquarters, Sao Paulo: pl. 39. Courtesy Mauro Warchavchik: fig. 15. Stuart Wrede: pls. 15, 17.

Contents

Foreword 6
Stuart Wrede

Preface 7

Roberto Burle Marx: The Unnatural Art of the Garden 8
William Howard Adams

Projects 39
- Early Drawings and Projects 40
- Private Gardens 46
- Gardens for the Workplace 60
- Public Gardens 68

Bibliography 78

Trustees of The Museum of Modern Art 80

Foreword

In 1964, The Museum of Modern Art published Elizabeth Kassler's *Modern Gardens and the Landscape*, a small but important book in which she sought to bring together the modern movement's finest achievements in landscape design from the 1920s through the early 1960s. The projects, although few in number, clearly define a modern landscape sensibility and grapple successfully with serious formal and aesthetic issues. In the mid-1960s, the course of landscape design began to shift as social and environmental concerns took precedence and designers found themselves creating pedestrian malls and children's playgrounds and addressing ecological issues. Although in hindsight aesthetic concerns and issues of a social and environmental nature need not be mutually exclusive, that seems to have been the result.

Today there is renewed interest in landscape design as a serious artistic endeavor. A new generation is picking up where an earlier one left off. Nevertheless, some of the most significant work done since 1964 has been completed by designers featured in Kassler's book, among them the Brazilian artist-gardener Roberto Burle Marx, who was instrumental in defining a modern landscape aesthetic in the late 1930s and who has continued to practice and refine his art to the present day.

It is particularly fitting, then, that The Museum of Modern Art should organize an exhibition of his landscape designs. Like his fellow Latin American Luis Barragán, whose work was featured in an exhibition at the Museum in 1972, Burle Marx stands out as one of the great designers in the field. Although Barragán, himself an architect, designed his gardens around architectural elements—chiefly walls—the raw materials for Burle Marx are earth and plants. A consummate plantsman, as William Howard Adams makes clear, Burle Marx has, over his long career, demonstrated that artistic and ecological concerns are in fact not mutually exclusive. His active efforts to save the Brazilian rain forest and its plant species (many of which have been incorporated into his gardens) predate by a generation or two this important and currently "fashionable" cause. On behalf of The Museum of Modern Art, I wish to express my gratitude to Burle Marx, who, still irrepressibly active at age eighty-one, has given his enthusiastic support and cooperation to this exhibition.

It has been a great pleasure to work with William Howard Adams, the exhibition's guest curator. Author of numerous books and articles on landscape, he brings deep knowledge and a broad historical perspective to the subject. As a Jefferson scholar par excellence, he also brings a classicist's critical eye to the field of modern landscape design.

Finally, we are most grateful for the generosity of the Banco Safra of Brazil in sponsoring this exhibition. The enlightened patronage of the institution has resulted in two of Burle Marx's most important gardens. To Mr. and Mrs. Gustavo Cisneros we are doubly grateful: first for underwriting research travel and a new set of photographs of the gardens and parks, and second for their indispensable help in marshalling support to make the exhibition a reality. Israel Klabin and Mrs. Donald B. Straus provided valuable advice at critical moments along the way. In addition, I would like to thank The International Council of The Museum of Modern Art for its encouragement and assistance, and for having made possible my trip to Brazil to meet with Burle Marx and see the gardens first hand.

Stuart Wrede
Director, Department of Architecture and Design

Preface

The very nature of the garden places it outside the museum gallery; its ephemeral, fugitive qualities and transient beauty are not susceptible to second-hand translation in plans, photographs, and models. It is reasonable then to question an exhibition that attempts to convey even a suggestion of the work of an artist who has chosen the garden as his chief medium of expression. Roberto Burle Marx—Brazilian painter, muralist, sculptor, architect, and set designer—decided at the beginning of his career that his true calling was the shaping of the natural topography into a work of art. It is on his terms, as an artist, that this effort has been made.

Many Burle Marx gardens never got beyond the drawing board. Of those that have been completed, a large number have disappeared or been poorly maintained, a hazard in gardening, where crucial lines, colors, and textures are dependent on keeping nature under control. Most of the gardens and parks featured in the exhibition and illustrated here were selected because it was possible to photograph them properly, which Michael Moran has done admirably.

Since most of Burle Marx's gardens are in South America, for many people their memories of the images seen on the walls of The Museum of Modern Art will be as close as they will come to the actual experience of walking through one of his creations. Whatever I may have conveyed of that experience is in large part due to the artist's guidance of my investigation. It is to him that I record my public thanks for his generosity of time and unfailing civility.

My preparations were also greatly aided by Denise Otis, a mutual friend of Roberto's and mine and a careful student of his work. She made available many source documents for my use. When Burle Marx was invited to the Museum some three years ago and the idea of an exhibition was first broached by Stuart Wrede, Director of the Department of Architecture and Design, Burle Marx was accompanied by a long-time colleague, the landscape architect Conrad Hamerman. A number of early plans by Burle Marx had been rescued by Hamerman, and he readily agreed to make them available for the exhibition. Since the fragile reality of garden art often extends to its preparatory drawings and models, which seem to share the evanescent character of the genre, future scholars will be deeply in Hamerman's debt, as are those of us who have worked on this exhibition.

In Burle Marx's office in Rio de Janeiro, his partner of twenty years, Haruyoshi Ono, whose imagination and hand are vital parts of the collaboration, has been of enormous assistance. It was also our good fortune to have had the help of Paulo Machado, a young Brazilian architect on his staff, who has carried out special research for both the exhibition and this catalog.

Without the steady encouragement and collaboration of Stuart Wrede, the exhibition would not have been possible. To members of the staff of The Museum of Modern Art, and especially to Matilda McQuaid, Assistant Curator in the Department of Architecture and Design, I express my gratitude for their diligence and help. Stuart Wrede, Denise Otis, Steven Krog, and Conrad Hamerman read the manuscript and made many valuable suggestions. They, of course, bear no responsibility for any lapses or misstatements that remain.

Elizabeth Howard oversaw the manuscript in many guises before it reached the editing stage. My neighbor Nicole Szulc Sachs provided me with translations from the Portuguese of a number of essays and articles.

Finally, I would like to thank the Myrin Institute for its continuing support of my work.

W.H.A.
October 1990

ROBERTO BURLE MARX: The Unnatural Art of the Garden

PART I

The Artist in Situ

Art springs from personality so it is only to personality that it can be revealed. —Oscar Wilde

It is about seven o'clock on a summer evening in Brazil. Roberto Burle Marx sits next to me on a bench as we lean back on the whitewashed wall of an old fazenda manor house to admire his latest garden creation. A storm has rolled down from the surrounding blue mountains and pauses briefly. The shower brightens the leaves of the bromeliads on the edge of the terrace steps. Burle Marx is savoring the dramatic twilight backlighting the garden, suddenly a romantic stage set. "If I am asked what is the most important natural factor in the design of a garden," he once remarked, "I think I must say it is light. Its constant change and capriciousness makes my work the most difficult—and the most satisfying." The garden designed for his friend Clemente Gomes at Fazenda Vargem Grande, located in a remote corner of the State of São Paulo, comes close to being number three thousand in a long list of works, both built and unbuilt over the past fifty-six years. Putting aside his Flamengo Park in Rio de Janeiro and the spectacular Copacabana beachfront, with its ribbon of black, white, and red mosaic waves, this garden may well be his finest achievement to date. In his lifetime, he has raised garden craft to a fine art, establishing, for all of its unpredictable variety, as the historian Michael Lancaster has pointed out, *o estilo Burle Marx*, a powerful style that can be compared favorably with the great garden designs of earlier centuries.

At eighty-one years of age, a measure of time that has little to do with the level of his creative energy, Roberto studies the garden with satisfaction (fig. 1). Melancholy light and deep shadows once more transform the garden, creating another in a series of moods that appear and then dissolve in the tropical atmosphere throughout the day. "Clouds and rain can change the focus of a garden; its whole proportion can be altered when the reflection disappears, or when a sudden storm leaves water in unaccustomed places." With a signal from a hidden prompter's box somewhere in the giant philodendron, sound is added to the light show, a steady beat like the beginning of a Japanese koda-drum performance. After the rhythm is established with a sharp, metallic throb, a deep baritone voice, now clearly recognizable as that of a frog, takes up a contrapuntal aria, followed closely by a full but modulated chorus. Burle Marx is obviously pleased by the impromptu *son et lumière* and joins the chorus with his own rich baritone.

"They seem to like my garden," he muses. "Gardens need more than flowers and plants. They need music and sound. That is one reason I love this garden—the sound of running water is always with us." As the water pours through openings and falls at irregular levels from the three terraces reaching up the hillside, it has different tones, rhythms, and volumes. Water is the central element at Fazenda Vargem Grande and has allowed Burle Marx to indulge his passion for every kind of water plant from not only Brazil but all over the world. His early international fame rests on his introduction of exotic plants collected throughout Brazil, and particularly in the jungle of the Amazon Basin, to garden design. On the two-hundred-foot terraces of Vargem Grande, with its pools and cascades, there is ample room for a brilliant orchestration of reflected texture and color on a scale inconceivable to a North American.

References to the structure and elements of music have played an important role in shaping

Fig. 1. Roberto Burle Marx in the garden of Fazenda Vargem Grande, Areira, São Paulo, 1990

Roberto's imagination as a garden designer. "One may even think of a plant as a note. Played in one chord, it will sound in a particular way; in another chord, its value will be altered. It can be legato, staccato, loud or soft, played on a tuba or on a violin. But it is the same note." Music has always been a part of his life, and it is never far from the surface when he is working at his office, puttering in his plant collection at home outside Rio, or sitting at the dinner table of a friend. Clemente Gomes shares the same irrepressible and often irreverent pleasure in music and joins Burle Marx in a fragment from a Gregorian Mass prompted by the servant's bell rung between courses while we are eating in the great kitchen. One night a mention of the celebrated Brazilian soprano Bidu Sayão inspires him to perform an affectionate falsetto imitation.

In his youth, Burle Marx had thought of becoming a professional singer, a career encouraged by his cultivated Brazilian mother, who had passed along to her son her own considerable musical talents. There are obvious musical qualities in his garden designs, both in their often flowing lines and in their harmony of color and form, not unlike the lyrical qualities in works of Matisse, where the abstract configurations of form and space express the artist's intentions. It is not an original observation, and when I mention it to him during one of our walks at the Fazenda Vargem Grande, he says he would agree if I mean the element of surprise encountered, say, in a chamber composition by Debussy, where you never quite know what is coming next. Then he hums an obscure passage to underline his point.

Pressing Roberto for his sources of inspiration in art, literature, garden history, or music will often set off a lively discourse on any one of these themes without revealing anything specific about his own complex process of arriving at what he calls "a creative solution." "I am an artist and I approach a garden design in that role. Not just as a painter," he quickly adds, "because the garden involves those dimensions of time and space that must be dealt with literally and not as an illusion on canvas." This respect for the elements and the demands of his craft as a gardener distinguishes his method of working as compared to the romantic myth of artistic "inspiration." His deep understanding of the life cycle of the enormous repertoire of plants he uses in his gardens is a part of his genius that few modern landscape architects and garden designers have. His knowledge of nature's mutability in form, color, and mood instills his mature creations with a special beauty that only he seems to have fully anticipated. The advantage of making gardens in the tropics is that the skeptics and critics—and he has had his share—do not have to wait long to see what he had in mind. The particular advantage of Brazil to Burle Marx's work has of course been the country's stupendous richness in native flora, numbering more than 50,000 species, an incalculable natural resource for an artist of his imagination, combined as it is with his botanist's flair for identifying the rare and unusual.

When talking about his early years and influences, he often says that he was blessed with a remarkably cultivated family with strong ties to Europe. His father, Wilhelm Marx, was born in Trier, Germany, the same town where Karl Marx was born. Biographical sketches have the families related in varying degrees, and he says that his father assumed some distant family connection. Roberto, who was born in São Paulo on August 4, 1909, speaks German along with at least five other languages and recalls that his father, who settled in Brazil in 1895, wisely insisted that the family speak only German at the dinner table. Santo Antonio da Bica, Burle Marx's garden estate near Rio, is famous for its good food and wine, and one night an interesting plum-colored wine produced at Trier followed the dessert, accompanied by an appropriate toast to his father's German roots.

It was his "mad" mother from the State of Pernambuco—her antecedents French and Dutch—who, with a gift of some plants and a small garden plot, introduced him to gardening as a child, about the same time she was teaching him the leitmotif from Wagner's *Tristan und Isolde*. Around 1913, Cecilia Burle Marx had taken a house in Leme, then a suburb of Rio at the end of the Copacabana Beach, where she developed her own large garden running up the

Morro da Babilonia to the forest and where Roberto had his first taste of the serious routines of gardening. It was in 1928, when he was nineteen, that Roberto traveled with his family to Germany, living there for a year and a half, to study music and painting. In Berlin he discovered the Dahlem Botanic Garden, where the hothouses held a collection of rare Brazilian plants. A year later, he returned to Rio (fig. 2), and in 1930 enrolled in the Escola Nacional de Belas Artes, the Rio school of fine arts, to study painting, architecture, and landscape design. Like other first-year art students at the school, Roberto also studied architecture (at the same time students of architecture studied painting), putting him in touch with young avant-garde architects. Through his friend Lucio Costa, who was briefly head of the school, he met fledgling architects Oscar Niemeyer, Jorge Machado Moreira, Gregori Warchavchik, and the brothers Marcelo and Milton Roberto, a group that would soon put Brazil in the forefront of the international modern movement. Another important influence was the great botanist Henrique Lahmeyer de Mello Barreto, head of Rio's zoological garden, who became his mentor. It was Barreto who deepened Roberto's knowledge of Brazilian plants on long botanical trips into the interior.

Fig. 2. Roberto Burle Marx. *Self-Portrait*, Rio de Janeiro, 1929. Charcoal, 18 1/2 x 12 1/4 in. (47 x 31 cm). Collection the artist

When Burle Marx is not working in his Rio office or traveling to new garden sites as far away as Florida and Pennsylvania, he will be found at Santo Antonio da Bica, Campo Grande, his old estate some nineteen miles south of the city, where he maintains his own private gardens and his fabled tropical plant collection, one of the most important in the world. The collection now belongs to a foundation supported by the government. It is here at Campo Grande that he continues to paint and to make an occasional garden sculpture as well as work in his incomparable botanical laboratory and studio.

At his house one day when it was too hot to do anything else, he suggested that we drive over to Bostos Tigre, a new roadside development on the road to Rio, where he had just completed a sculpture for a small community park (fig. 3). Ever since 1934, when Burle Marx had moved to Recife in northeastern Brazil to spend

Fig. 3. Roberto Burle Marx. Playground sculpture, Bostos Tigre, Rio de Janeiro, 1990. Painted concrete, 32 ft. 1 7/8 in. (1000 cm) high

two years as Keeper of Parks for the State of Pernambuco, public parks have been an important part of his design legacy (see plates 2–9). Beginning in 1954, he had been occupied by the creation of Flamengo Park on an enormous landfill curving around Guanabara Bay in the heart of Rio and incorporating the Santos Dumont Airport (for which he designed a garden in 1938) and the Museu de Arte Moderno (plates 54, 55). Copacabana Beach of 1970 (plates 56–58), the park most familiar to tourists, extends from the sand to the very entrance of the long blocks of hotels fronting the ocean. The pattern of the nearly four-mile-long, boldly abstract, mosaic walkway of black, milk-white, and Venetian-red stone was adapted from an old decorative pavement used in seventeenth-century Lisbon. The Parque del Este of 1956–61, in Caracas, Venezuela, is one of the larger projects, although it was never completed: Burle Marx's grand visions respect neither politicians nor budgets.

The new park, Bostos Tigre, only a half hour from his house, is on a dusty, flat, village block located on a nondescript stretch of highway. Behind a temporary construction wall, raised on short steel piers, stands a bold, abstract composition, cast in concrete, some thirty feet high and painted in the primary colors of red, yellow, and blue. The first version of the park plan followed its own configurations of harmony to play against the dominating sculpture. When a revised version of the park was produced during my stay in Rio de Janeiro, I had an opportunity to glimpse something of the working process of the office. The quiet tensions of creative concentration were palpable as Roberto Burle Marx and his partner, Haruyoshi Ono, worked together on the alternative plan for the little park.

The office, which began in the family house in Leme, now occupies a turn-of-the-century house near the center of Rio in a quiet hillside quarter called Laranjeiras, the Portuguese for Orange Grove. A small parlor has been converted to a conference room, and the old dining room still functions as the place for the staff's midday meal, with Roberto at the head of the table. Overlooking the back garden is a large work room filled with eight drafting tables and lined with standing rows of brown-cardboard tubes that hold completed plans. When a new project comes into the office, everyone is invited to participate in the initial discussions with an easy, open, give and take. For young architects and interns this is heady stuff. Burle Marx, of course, works closely with Ono, but he listens to all ideas and suggestions that surface. The client for the new park is developing housing nearby and feels some recreation facilities are called for, so a small play area is worked into the scheme, a change that seems right and does not appear to disrupt Roberto's setting for his startling new and experimental sculpture.

The capital city of Brasília, begun in 1956 on the high savanna of the western country, was the largest landscaping opportunity to date in a country where massive public works had long been a national tradition. Yet in the beginning international critics believed the regime of President Juscelino Kubitschek, sponsor of the new city in the wilderness, had neglected to invite Brazil's most famous landscape designer to participate. Some thought it was because the artist found Lucio Costa's master plan for the city outdated, an example of nineteenth-century utopianism. Others suspected that Burle Marx had little sympathy for Oscar Niemeyer's indulgent, pseudomodern buildings. But according to Grady Clay in *Landscape Architecture* (1963), Burle Marx belatedly became involved in Brasília following Kubitschek's defeat in 1961. The artist had turned down an earlier invitation to participate because Kubitschek, as mayor of Belo Horizonte, a new town created in the 1930s, had failed to pay for work Burle Marx had done for that city.

In landscape work, Burle Marx has brought his skills as a scientist into symbiotic play with his creative, artistic imagination. Nearly twenty years ago he spoke of the relationship between gardens and ecology, referring to the need for an understanding of the natural environment but defending the artist's response to its requirements as crucial to a man-made design in the landscape. Although he may admire certain aspects of natural gardening and the perennial attempts to recreate the illusion of nature in urban parks and suburban subdivisions, his philosophy and vision are guided by the sensibility of an artist whose work rejects meaning based on serviceability or historical context and reference. The new water garden at the Fazenda Vargem Grande was carefully worked out in detailed drawings as early as 1979, eight years before planting began. What is remarkable, however, is to see how few changes and improvisations there were between the original plan (plate 27) and the completed garden itself. The methods of representing garden designs are not the same as those for architecture, where elevations, facades, and photographs along with plans indicate the finished space. Yet Burle Marx's knowledge of plants and their life cycles enables him to anticipate the mature, organic, three-dimensional composition from the abstraction of plans alone. The result is scarcely less formal than a Cubist painting or a Beaux-Arts *parti*. The mysterious and unexpected intimacies encountered in the garden are not the result of undifferentiated plant material being placed on a hillside nor of a superficial preoccupation with spectacular and compelling views of mountains and bucolic meadows. Rather, they recall a classical landscape by Poussin, an artist I thought of more than once while contemplating Roberto's composition. The consecutive and contemporaneous sequences of general views are reinforced with the richest details of flowers and specific textures of leaves—banishing all monotony in this large space—much as one might imagine a stroll in one of Poussin's landscape paintings. William Wordsworth's reflection on Poussin captures their effect: "the unity that pervades them, the superintending mind, the imaginative principle that brings all to bear on the same end." The bifurcation of one's perceptions, moving constantly between the specific and the general, between a spray of delicate, long-stemmed orchids and a sudden panorama of the valley below, is an example of Burle Marx's carefully considered aesthetic and ecological contributions to garden art, combining the sensual pleasures of space with the equally sensual pleasures of nature. "A work of art," he has often remarked, "cannot be the result of a haphazard solution."

Several times during my stay at Vargem Grande we talked about the state of landscape design. He could not understand why so few landscape architects consider themselves artists or view their work as an art form. And, although many in American landscape-gardening circles would think it heresy, Roberto believes that students should be trained in the Beaux-Arts tradition of draftsmanship, that they should draw in order to sharpen their powers of observation. On Sundays apprentice members of his staff turn up at Campo Grande to sketch details of the plants and flowers. When a couple of young garden designers from abroad came to visit without their sketchbooks, he was privately critical of them.

Still, Burle Marx has remained true to the modern movement in art and architecture and acknowledges the influence of the rigorous polemics of Le Corbusier and Walter Gropius. When Le Corbusier came to Brazil in 1936 and sketched out plans for the Ministry of Education and Health in Rio, he was asked to produce designs for the landscape work (plate 34). One of his closest friends was the Brazilian modern architect Rino Levi, whose rational, elegant buildings were almost inevitably enhanced by a Burle Marx garden. Nor was he expected to provide merely a decorative setting for an aggressive piece of modern architecture. The original garden and park designed in 1950 for the home of Olivo Gomes at São José dos Campos (plates 18–22), a modern country house by Levi, is one of the most satisfying contemporary collaborations between an architect and landscape designer, where each artist worked to complement the other.

Although the materials of landscape (vegetation, water, soil, rocks) have not changed with technology, Roberto has sought out exotic plant forms that can interact with and comment on the surrounding high-tech settings he is forced to deal with, as he did to great effect in the dry roof garden of the Safra Bank in São Paulo (plates 37–39). A neighboring building gutted by fire seems an appropriate if unexpected backdrop. Vertical fern trees repeat the lines of the skyscrapers nearby.

It is tropical twilight now as we sit on the long, low veranda of Santo Antonio da Bica—

Fig. 4. Plant shed, Santo Antonio da Bica, the Burle Marx country home at Campo Grande, Rio de Janeiro

Saint Anthony of the Spring. The acid magenta of the orchids comes up in the dim light against the gray garden wall Burle Marx has constructed out of fragments of granite from Victorian buildings ruthlessly pulled down in Rio. The house is low, single-storied, with the deep veranda running along the valley side where you can look down into a rectilinear pool. Farther down the slope is a vast plant shed (fig. 4) covered by black netting held in place by bamboo slats. Inside is his (and Brazil's) great collection of bromeliads, calatheas, philodendrons, anthuriums, and heliconias. On sea-worn boulders around and above the house are other Brazilian plants: cactus, orchids, palms, and more bromeliads. I am reminded that nearly forty years ago Burle Marx sounded the tocsin to arouse Brazil and the world to the threatened devastation of the native flora in the virgin forests of the Amazon and to our new capacity to destroy in an hour the labor of thousands of years of evolution. Because of our carelessness, greed, or what he would call "a want of culture," we slide toward annihilation, and more than primitive flora will be lost.

We go into dinner passing in the hallway the botanical watercolors of Roberto's friend Margaret Mee, recording rare and unknown species called *burle-marxii*, in honor of their discoverer. I tell him of Albert Einstein's bequest to Princeton for his beloved trees, which had given the scientist so much pleasure. Emotion rises in his eyes. "'The trees of Princeton'—beautiful," he whispers, and then he recalls that his mother accompanied Einstein's violin, adding that he played it badly. Someone mentions Richard Strauss. Immediately we are introduced to some complex passages from *Elektra*. César, the most sophisticated chef in Brazil, sets his banquet on a vibrant tablecloth Roberto has painted. For a brief moment everyone is able to put aside the political issues of Brazil and the future of the tropical plant foundation Roberto created to preserve a lifetime of collecting. Tomorrow a load of bromeliads will leave from the private nursery for the new water garden at the Fazenda Vargem Grande. And for a brief moment the world seems on the verge of returning to the path of civility and, yes, cultivation.

PART II

The Unnatural Art of the Garden

A garden is the result of an arrangement of natural materials according to aesthetic laws; interwoven throughout are the artist's outlook on life, his past experiences, his affections, his attempts, his mistakes, and his successes. —Roberto Burle Marx

Transforming the craft of gardening into art is an alchemy that has seldom been achieved in this century. The base ingredients of plants, soil, water, rocks, and sunlight are common enough in spite of our efforts to destroy them, but the creative agents and reagents necessary to effect the change have somehow lost much of their potency. It is difficult to name even a handful of artists who have dedicated their imagination and skill to the art of the garden and the landscape. Lucio Costa, Burle Marx's earliest mentor, advised his student not to call himself a "gardener," perhaps realizing how little respect and encouragement one could expect from architects, whose ambitions set the course and often overwhelmed the direction of modern landscape design. But Burle Marx was determined to "use the natural topography as a field of work and the elements of nature, mineral and vegetable, as materials for plastic construction, as other artists worked on canvas with paint and brush."[1]

From the beginning of Burle Marx's career, an important ingredient of his success has been his willingness to accept as an artist the unpredictable and experimental conditions of his chosen field. He was also armed with a critical intelligence equal to his particular vision of the garden as a work of art. Art would be his means of bringing nature's primal coarseness under control, giving it proportion, limits, and beauty that man could live with and enjoy. From the moment man intervenes in the natural landscape, rules of order and organization must be devised to prevent hopeless chaos, and that should be the job of the gardener. Burle Marx, unlike many contemporary landscape designers, is unabashed by nature, never hesitating to intrude upon its province. Nor has he been uneasy with applying an artist's sense of order, although such an unease has compromised many designers of this century.

Having freed himself from dependence on the architectural setting as the decisive element in garden design, Burle Marx made a daring effort to come to terms with those same forces that have reshaped art and architecture in the modern world. His very definition of a garden, having a heroic, even tragic bias, lifts it above what architectural historian Joseph Rykwert, in an essay that has broadened the subject of garden design beyond the provincial, calls "a fringe phenomenon."[2] It was not in Adam's hut, after all, but in a garden that man first defined and modified his universe by asserting his humanity over the landscape.

The array of new techniques in landscape design—environmental planning, demographic research to determine the size of recreational facilities, traffic engineering, formulas for allotting parking space in shopping malls—may be efficient craftsmanship, but the ends they achieve are often dubious and encourage the mindless proliferation of man-made objects throughout the environment. These techniques have had little to do with resolving aesthetic issues of garden design, which was conceived as a form of art on a level with painting, sculpture, and architecture, at a time when the garden was still an important aspect of civilization. At the turn of the century, as architects searched for new theories, ideals, and materials in an effort to throw off inherited eclecticism, most garden designers, or landscape architects—the label the the new American professionals adopted—clung to the past either in its revived Continental dress or as a verdant dream of the English picturesque. By the 1890s, variations of these park and garden fashions had spread to the urban centers of both North and South America, where new Italianate villas were surrounded by Renaissance Revival parterres. Nearby parks attempted to affect the curving drives and romantic tree clumps *au naturel* of the eighteenth-century international style made famous by Lancelot Brown and Humphry Repton. When the American landscape gardener Frederick Law Olmsted was received in London in 1892, the protagonists in the battle between the formal and informal schools had gone public with their controversy. Sir Reginald Blomfield, a leading Beaux-Arts architect, insisted on "a complete return to the old formal gardening," while the Irish gardener William Robinson crankily spoke for a laissez-faire naturalism in an attempt to blur all distinctions between the natural and the man-made.[3] Surprisingly, Olmsted sided with the architect.

With the establishment of academic programs in landscape design in the first decade of this century, endemic eclecticism was replaced, as the critic and landscape architect Steven Krog has written, by a preoccupation with bolstering "the status of the nascent discipline among competing professions."[4] Norman Newton, writing in 1932, expressed the widely held view that "the landscape architect must devote his energies to the application of changeless principles to our changing mode of living: the question of 'modern' or 'not modern' will take care of itself."[5] Thus the debate over the future course of landscape design during the formative years of Burle Marx's career was more concerned with the relative merits of competing yet outmoded garden styles and journalistic fashions disguised as "changeless principles" than with addressing the issues raised by those demanding a new art and architecture. *Landscape Architecture*, the journal of the American Society of Landscape Architects, founded in 1899, regularly featured articles on Italian, French, and English historical styles to reassure a new profession eager to associate itself with European traditions and standards.

Even though landscape architects were called upon to deal with a wide spectrum of problems related to the environment and urban growth after the turn of the century, there emerged no new theory and few experiments comparable to those in the field of architecture. The Art Nouveau movement had urged a return to nature as the source of inspiration embracing all design, yet with little lasting impact on garden layouts. For most modern movement architects, the extent of their dreams of landscape was to see their skyscrapers standing in the middle of an English park—Olmsted's picturesque Central Park of 1857 seems prescient in this regard. But in the years just before the First World War, a few critics in Vienna began to speak in visionary tones of a new concept of garden art that would conquer nature in its bold simplicity, suggesting a complete break with the past. Out of this idealistic if vague philosophy would emerge a new garden aesthetic based on and "open to," according to Secessionist architect Joseph Olbrich, "new sensibilities and new ideas."[6] In 1909 Joseph August Lux declared in the Viennese journal *Der Architekt*: "Garden art is the most notable and happiest negation of wild nature," going on to predict that art will "create an antithesis to nature in the garden . . . following architectural principles which strengthen the expression of human illusion."[7] The Viennese architect Josef Hoffmann projected a new geometry in his plans for the garden of the Palais Stoclet, Brussels, in 1905, closely integrating it into the architecture. The Stoclet garden, severely architectonic, was to have a profound influence on the young Belgian architect Robert Mallet-Stevens, who saw it as it was being built.

In 1928, when the nineteen-year-old Burle Marx left Rio de Janeiro with his family to spend a year in Weimar Germany, only a few Europeans were aware of the garden as an artistic medium. Most of the experimental work was concentrated in and around Paris, where efforts were made to find an analogue to express in landscape design the new ideas now visible in modern painting and sculpture. French garden designer André Véra, working with his brother Paul, a member of a Cubist group, designed a garden in the contemporary idiom at Place des États-Unis, Paris, in 1926 (fig. 5). In its fractured space and mirrored wall, it was a significant if tentative step, but in retrospect it is difficult to see this or an earlier project by Mallet-Stevens, the garden for the villa Les Roses Rouges of 1914, as being as modern or as revolutionary as some have claimed. The faceted, Cubist lines gave it a static, bijoulike quality that a garden needs to avoid.

The first garden to make a dramatic break with the established traditions of spatial and compositional arrangement came in 1925 at the Exposition des Arts Décoratifs in Paris.

Fig. 5. André and Paul Véra. Triangular garden, Hôtel de Noailles, Paris, 1926. Photograph by Man Ray

Armenian designer Gabriel Guévrékian, from the Josef Hoffmann atelier in Vienna, had joined Mallet-Stevens in Paris, where he was invited to produce a garden design for the Exposition. Guévrékian's *Jardin d'eau et de lumière* represented, as historian Richard Wesley has pointed out, "the first experiment to elevate the aesthetic of garden design to the level of modern painting."[8] The Armenian designer's notoriety led the following year to a commission to design the garden for a modern villa Mallet-Stevens had created for Vicomte Charles de Noailles in 1927–28 near Hyères, in southwest France (fig. 6).

The immediate background of garden and landscape design in South America before the turn of

Fig. 6. Gabriel Guévrékian. Garden for Vicomte Charles de Noailles, Hyères, France, 1927–28

the century contained certain recognizable cultural similarities inherited from its European colonial past. But the tropical world of Brazil, so far removed from Europe, where history is etched into the topography, was utterly different. The modification of Brazil's incomparable natural landscape began with the arrival of the first Europeans in 1500 and continued through the destructive cycles of sugar and coffee production over the next three hundred and fifty years. Burle Marx has said that the most defining peculiarity of the Brazilian landscape outside the cities when he was a boy was charred, burned-over land being prepared for agricultural exploitation. "There appeared in the settler's mind a compulsion to open up strategic clearings and an urge to pull things down, to destroy."[9] By adopting and perpetuating these primitive techniques of nomadic agriculture and applying

Fig. 7. Auguste-François-Marie Glaziou. Campo de Sant'Ana, Rio de Janeiro, 1873–80. Photograph by Marc Ferrez, c. 1885

Fig. 8. Lake Frei Leandro, Jardim Botanico, Rio de Janeiro. Aspect of the garden containing indigenous plants of Brazil. Photograph by Marc Ferrez, c. 1890

advanced, imported technology, Burle Marx warned, we have the blind power to destroy countless millennia of nature's evolution.

In 1808 the beleaguered Portuguese monarch, Dom João VI, suddenly driven out of the home country by Napoleon, fled to his nation's colony in South America, bringing with him a mission of French scientists, engineers, and artists, who introduced new ideas from Europe into the urban landscape to impart an imperial tone. A botanical garden was established in Rio de Janeiro within a year of his arrival, in 1809, and a magnificent *allée* of Barbados royal palms brought from the West Indies was immediately planted. But most urban landscaping in nineteenth-century Brazilian cities was carried out with European trees and plants, viewed as being more prestigious and "civilized" by the émigré court.

By the time Burle Marx and his family had moved from São Paulo to Rio de Janeiro in 1913, the new parks, gardens, and boulevards of the latter half of the nineteenth century had attained a certain flamboyant panache in their quick, tropical maturity (figs. 7 and 8). For the most part these urban parks were colonial versions of European fashions for either formality or the picturesque. The English picturesque had arrived in Brazil with the distinct French accent of the imported civil engineers who took charge of laying out the new imperial boulevards and parks in the Brazilian capital. The style had

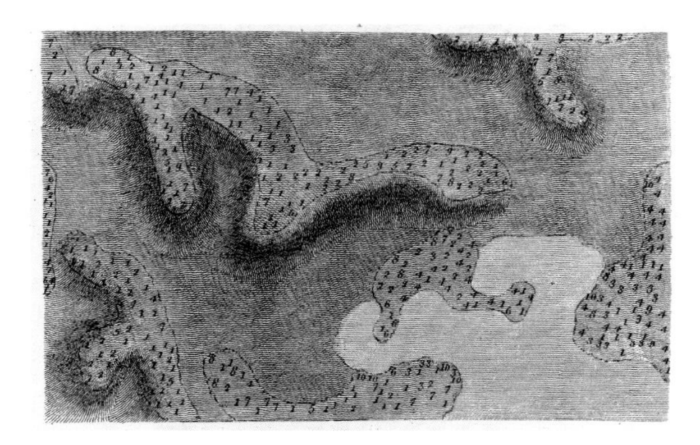

Fig. 9. John Claudius Loudon. Planting plan. Plate from *Treatise on Country Residences* (London, 1806)

Fig. 10. Winter garden, Jardin des Plantes, Paris. Plate from *Histoire des jardins anciens et modernes* (Paris, 1887), by Arthur Mangin

been introduced in France after the Revolution by Alexandre de Laborde in his *Nouveaux jardins de la France*, published in 1808. Laborde's interpretation of the picturesque was closely related to Humphry Repton's, but Repton's loose method of improvisation was quickly rationalized into a typically French formula of crisply defined, conventional drives with ample curves, molded dells in the middle of lawns, and massive clumps of decorative horticulture. Later, Jean-Charles-Adolphe Alphand and his followers would extend the influence of their landscape engineering of circular, oval, and elliptical lines, seen in the public parks of Paris but far removed from the English origins, well into the twentieth century. There was also the "gardenesque" style, translated into tropical exuberance from English and French models. Evolved from the writings of the English garden publicist John Claudius Loudon, the gardenesque style had been enthusiastically embraced by Victorians on both sides of the Atlantic. Loudon, who had invented the label, insisted in his definition that the design of the garden should be consciously artificial, "calculated for displaying the art of the gardener" (fig. 9).[10] Its artificiality was necessary to distinguish a garden as a work of art rather than as an inconsequential exercise in "picturesque," a concept Loudon had apparently picked up from the early nineteenth-century writings of the Frenchman A.-C. Quatremère de Quincy.

Quatremère had also promoted the extensive use of foreign rather than native plants in gardens and parks as a way of giving them greater artistic verisimilitude. With the gardenesque's high standards of botanical knowledge and intellectual discipline, it followed the ambitions of nineteenth-century Empire, as exotic new flowers and trees poured into Great Britain and Europe from all over the world. Public and private botanical gardens sprang up in Berlin, London, Paris (fig. 10), and many other cities to celebrate the new colonial conquests. Former European colonies from the Subcontinent and Africa to the continents of the Americas also reversed the international horticultural exchange by importing European plants and trees that could for the first time be safely transported halfway around the world. Such figures as Henry Winthrop Sargent, a wealthy American horticulturalist, assembled a magnificent collection of imported aloe and cactus for the greenhouse at his Hudson River estate not long after the Civil War. It was this adventurous scientific and botanical curiosity, made possible by nineteenth-century technology, that also encouraged centers like the Dahlem Botanic Garden in Berlin to collect Brazilian plants, which the young Burle Marx would discover during his first visit to Europe. The very exuberance of the Brazilian flora, seen in the bleak light of a German winter, induced Burle Marx to study the language of plants, using his native vocabulary to enrich its poetry. The English roses, carnations, chrysanthemums, dahlias, and cinerarias that proliferated in his mother's fashionable garden in the suburbs of Rio may also have stirred his early determination to move in the opposite horticultural direction.

Added to the setting in the Rio of Roberto's childhood was a special Brazilian decadence, where too much was considered in the best of taste, giving native craftsmen license to overdo everything with decorative excess. Only the label Art Nouveau gave it respectability. It was at this time that there began the relentless destruction of older Brazilian architecture, along with gardens and parks, and the trend gained momentum in the 1930s and 1940s. The few scattered pockets of decaying history that are now left give the streets of Rio and São Paulo a disjointed, decomposed appearance. Fragments of some of these buildings were rescued by Roberto and incorporated into the garden at Santo Antonio da Bica beginning in 1949.

This period of parvenue development saw the spread of the ubiquitous suburban bungalows, accompanied, in Burle Marx's words, by "overtall sickly conifers." These garden fashions extended well into the 1930s, reinforced by American-influenced magazines published in Brazil. The gardens featured in these magazines were attempts to replicate their North American cousins. Native plants were not a part of these imported compositions, even though the botanical garden in Rio de Janeiro had in fact established a large collection of South American flora through the efforts of a long line of distinguished Brazilian botanists.

The sensual, painterly line Burle Marx developed and clarified in his garden designs of the 1940s and 1950s, with their interlocking forms of planting beds, walks, pools, and screen walls, reveals his affinity for abstract art of the time. Images by Arp, Calder, Léger, Miró, and Picasso are hinted at and then transformed in the dynamics of his compositions. These artists were collected in South America, and in the case of Arp, Calder, and Léger, were given major commissions. Architects were also experimenting with free forms suggesting biological analogies that were not unlike some of the amoeboid imagery of the Surrealists. "Nature, biology, has rich and luxuriant forms," Alvar Aalto declared in 1935,[11] later giving tangible expression to this observation in the amoeboid swimming pool of the Villa Mairea in 1938 and in the curving lines of the Finnish pavilion at the New York World's Fair of 1939. Given the sensitivity of Burle Marx to the art of this century, this shared vocabulary is not surprising. It is important, however, to understand that these forms were transformed in the process, so that the result is not merely "painting with plants," as some critics have suggested.

Burle Marx's precision of line also suggests a reinvented, romantic awareness of the earlier landscape work of Auguste-François-Marie Glaziou, a French hydraulic engineer and botanist, who designed the Campo de Sant'Ana park in Rio between 1873 and 1880 (see fig. 7). "When, in 1934, I started to lay out gardens," Roberto recalls, "it was still possible, in a few Glaziou gardens, to find the traces of the master's hand, of a man who knew plants, and how they could be made into a garden."[12] Glaziou had been educated in Paris, where he became familiar with the work of Jean-Charles-Adolphe Alphand, who had helped transform the Bois de Boulogne and other parks for Baron Haussmann in the middle of the nineteenth century. Alphand's landscapes of volutes and curves were widely circulated in *Les Promenades de Paris*, published between 1867 and 1873, among them the plan for the Parc des Buttes-Chaumont of 1869 (fig. 11), laid out in an abandoned quarry.

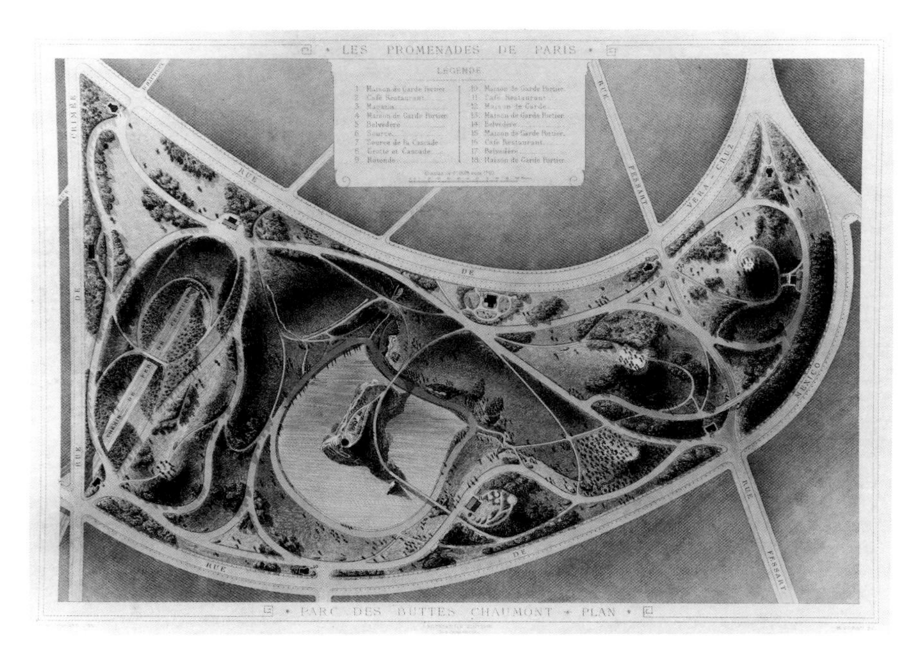

Fig. 11. Jean-Charles-Adolphe Alphand. Plan for Parc des Buttes-Chaumont, Paris, 1869. Plate from *Les Promenades de Paris* (c. 1873)

Setting a significant precedent for Roberto's own experiments, Glaziou made a number of plant-collecting expeditions into the hinterlands of Brazil and used the specimens collected in his Rio parks; but his curious and original introduction of natural boulders into the design of the Praça de Republica (fig. 12), begun in 1880, later became a major element in a number of projects by Burle Marx, who often taps the mineral kingdom for inspiration. The genealogy of the decorative use of rustic boulders in an artificial setting reaches back to the Renaissance, but Glaziou's predilection for them in the Praça de Republica can be linked to Alphand's inspired use of rocks and rock plants in the Parisian park of Buttes-Chaumont. Glaziou's delineation of the composition along sharply edged drives anticipated Burle Marx's similar concern for spatial definition, a consistent element in his design strategy. Throughout the Brazilian artist's work, there has always been not only this fascination with precision of line in controlling large areas of land but also a sensual preoccupation with the juxtaposition of disparate textures, materials, and colors that require the most intense skills of execution and maintenance, defying nature to rebut the artist's argument.

Fig. 12. Auguste-François-Marie Glaziou. Praça de Republica, Rio de Janeiro, c. 1880. Photograph by Marc Ferrez, c. 1885

Fig. 13. Copacabana Beach, Rio de Janeiro, view toward Morro do Leme. Photograph by Marc Ferrez, 1890

From the first settlement of Rio de Janeiro, its natural splendors of sea, mountains, and forest imposed themselves on the people's minds and emotions. Rio's aesthetic magnificence is overwhelming, entering the very psyche of its inhabitants. As many have observed, this now endangered ecosystem, home to nearly twelve million people, has been an inescapable condition for the creative work of Burle Marx. For all the city's pollution, urban sprawl, and appalling poverty, Rio remains an aphrodisiac, an inspiration combining what the Swiss naturalist Louis Agassiz called life's three most profound moments, when one "views the ocean, gazes upon a towering peak, and ventures into a tropical forest."[13]

The remains of Brazil's ancient Atlantic forests stretch down from the rocky slopes of the Serra do Mar coastal range, pushing around monumental, domed, stone barriers to reach the sea. In some of Rio's short cross streets running from the Copacabana Beach to the abrupt granite base of the mountain only a few blocks away, the forest vegetation seems to pour into the crowded thoroughfares like primordial lava. The powerful influence of this baroque stagedrop, with its mountain and coastal curves, inspired the landscape work of a number of Rio's engineer-designers in the nineteenth century (figs. 13 and 14). When in 1954 the architect Affonso Eduardo Reidy invited Burle Marx to design the new Flamengo Park (plate 53) on the landfill of Guanabara Bay, the undulating lines he laid down drew their vitality from the primitive surroundings that continue to dominate the heart of Rio.

For all the park's enormous scale, increased by reflecting water and monumental bare mountains of dark granite laced with dense fragments of old forests, the horticultural organization of the Burle Marx design is equal in strength to the natural setting, neither lost nor obscured in this landscape. The malleable quality that Burle Marx brings out in his compositions, as on a roof garden above Botafogo Bay or in the Odette Monteiro Garden (plates 14–17), enhancing a particular passage of color or plant group, somehow encourages our eyes to move from an intimate interlude to the larger orchestration of the mountain or cityscape beyond, without disrupting the unity. Burle Marx's biographer, Flavio Motta, isolates this elusive quality of the artist in a long and intense study of the landscape itself and quotes from a letter written from Rio in 1865 by Elizabeth Cary Agassiz, who identifies the same phenomenon:

The great charm of the landscape is that, for all of its vastness, it is never so distant as to make things lose their individuality. After all, what is a panorama seen from afar if not an inventory? So many patches of dark green, so many forests; so many strips of a lighter green, so many meadows, so many white puddles, so many lakes, so many silvery threads, so many rivers. . . . Here contrary to the expected, no partial effect is lost in the vastness of the whole.[14]

Fig. 14. Avenida Beira Mar, facing Botafogo Bay, Rio de Janeiro. Photograph by Marc Ferrez, 1906

In 1934 when Burle Marx moved to Recife to become head of public parks for the State of Pernambuco, advanced artistic and architectural experiments were already well underway in Brazil. Twelve years before, in 1922, a cultural and aesthetic revolution was announced at Modern Art Week, in São Paulo, an event featuring avant-garde exhibitions, lectures, and dance and music recitals. In 1925 Rino Levi, then an obscure architectural student studying in Rome, saw the connection between the first appearance of modern architecture in Brazil and events in Europe when he wrote a letter to a São Paulo newspaper: "The movement manifesting itself today in the arts and especially in architecture is worthy of note. Everything leads to the belief that a new era is about to begin, if it has not begun already."[15]

Much of this energy attracting talented young architects proclaiming the spirit of a new age came to be concentrated in the leadership of Lucio Costa, especially during his brief tenure as head of the Escola Nacional de Belas Artes in Rio. In 1932 Costa had secured for Roberto his first commission, a roof garden for the small, austere Alfredo Schwartz House (fig. 15), which Lucio Costa and Gregori Warchavchik, followers of Le Corbusier, had designed. Its white geometry of militant Bauhaus restraint demanded the vibrant, plastic setting that Burle Marx would eventually evolve through his manipulation of plants and vegetation. Because of his sophisticated horticultural knowledge, Burle Marx was taking a direction far different from anything proposed by contemporary architects or by garden designers in Europe. The most that Le Corbusier could come up with for the setting of his Villa Savoie in the suburbs of Paris was a romantic, pastoral campagna extracted from recollections of lines from Virgil, replete with grazing cows in tall grass.

Roberto's job in Recife was to revitalize the old dilapidated public parks and squares laid out in the nineteenth century. The sketches and drawings from this period (plates 2–10) reveal the intensity of his concentration on his newly invented language of plants, making expression of their scientific and aesthetic individuality his first priority rather than design or composition.

Fig. 15. Roberto Burle Marx. Roof garden of Alfredo Schwartz House, Rio de Janeiro, 1932

The Recife gardens themselves, many of them only remodeled, tended toward the geometric and academic. If modern-movement architects were testing new building materials of glass and reinforced concrete, wild plants from the mountains and deserts that had never before been used in gardens would be Roberto's raw material. Composition would follow after he had mastered the vocabulary of his new language. His aim would be to perfect a "technical feeling for nature . . . attained through science."[16] His scientific research would include plant-hunting expeditions to the rain forests in the Amazon valley and a long apprenticeship with the botanist Henrique Lahmeyer de Mello Barreto.

The metaphors of "vocabulary" and "language" have long provided critics with a convenient way to reduce all cultural productions, including gardens, to an intellectual "text" that can be easily read. But a caveat is called for. The visual experience of paintings, films, gardens, and architecture is easily translated into a "reading." Yet this convention can be highly limiting and misleading with an artist like Burle Marx, who caters first of all to the eye. As the critic Camille Paglia has pointed out, this moralistic obsession with text concentrates on the unseen and the abstract at the expense of the "eye-intense"[17] image itself. In the artist's visual exploitation of nature's incessant botanical themes, the analogies of text and language break down before the rush of the purely visual energy released. It is in this mastery of the living environmental substance of nature that Burle

Fig. 16. Roberto Burle Marx. Paláçio das Prinçesas (detail), Recife, Pernambuco, 1936. India ink on paper, 18 1/8 x 23 1/4 in. (46 x 59 cm)

Marx has been able to put the garden on an equal footing with the revolutionary advances of painting and architecture. If architecture could be an art, gardens could also provide something more than "functional solutions." As art critic Harold Rosenberg said of the painter Arshile Gorky, Burle Marx has lived "relentlessly forward" in his art, and has, like Gorky, used his aesthetic experience to anticipate "events-to-come peculiar to artists, gamblers, and prophets."[18]

Although the modern movement rejected the Beaux-Arts faith in drawing as integral to the creative process, the pencil, a reminder of official French taste, was revered at the school of fine arts in Rio for both artists and architects when Burle Marx began his studies there. The school was founded in 1820 and followed the philosophy of the French Academy in uniting painting, sculpture, and architecture. There were no courses in landscape design; the first one, in fact, was not offered until 1971. Le Corbusier the painter was sympathetic to the French tradition and had long kept sketchbooks. He continued to do so when he arrived in Rio to work with Lucio Costa and the latter's former students in 1936. Contemporary architects Louis Kahn, Carlo Scarpa, and Alvar Aalto also practiced this tradition of firsthand observation translated into spontaneous sketches. Burle Marx would have agreed with Scarpa when he declared: "I want to see, therefore I draw."[19]

The act of drawing has always been second nature to Burle Marx the painter, and in connection with his garden designs drawing has been the means to finding a solution or uncovering a new idea for a particular project or site plan. As he marshals his ideas in his head or on paper, there is always present that critical, accumulated knowledge of the plant material itself. This understanding includes a specimen's ecological grouping, habit of growth, color, texture, and the changing role of light he has so often spoken of. In the drawings from the Recife period, as in the Paláçio das Prinçesas (fig. 16), it is clear that the artist's first goal was the enlargement of his new vocabulary of plants. Palms of various species are tested for their ability to serve as columns and walls. The tectonic qualities of the papyrus and the Brazilian water-lily (*Victoria regis*) are closely studied on pools of water under different refractions of light and the movement of wind. There is the crucial measure of the bromeliads' ability to survive as living elements of architecture implanted in walls and terraces. Other families are tested for their reliability in and among rocks, a favorite juxtaposition of the artist. In a drawing of the Praça Euclides da Cunha, in Recife (plate 9),[20] he exploits the disquieting beauty of cactus plants he had first seen and studied in their native habitat, the arid desert of the Sertão in northeastern Brazil. The results of his more than fifty years of research and experimentation continue to be evident in his major works, as in the terraces of the new water garden at Fazenda Vargem Grande (fig. 17).

Le Corbusier's participation in the design of the Ministry of Education and Health (fig. 18)—

Fig. 17. Roberto Burle Marx. Water garden, Fazenda Vargem Grande, 1979–90

view. The flatness of the countryside has been relieved with lakes and mounds planted with tall grass, filling it with the poetic surprise and mystery of a painting by Corot. Here is architecture utterly at home in a rational domain of altered nature, conceived in every detail by the artist gardener.

Levi was commissioned to design a number of other buildings on the extensive Gomes property, projects in which Burle Marx was invited to participate. The only two buildings completed comprise the Parahyba Dairies plant of 1965, now abandoned, designed for processing milk and cheese and intended to have been part of a larger agro-industrial complex. A large industrial shed, complete with a filling station, is decorated with a ceramic-tile mural reminiscent of Léger but designed by Burle Marx. The vines and plants in the open atrium between the two factory units (fig. 22), long untended, now dematerialize the romantically decaying Miesian architecture.

By the 1950s Burle Marx began to explore a more geometric form of garden composition, beginning in 1952 with a rectilinear scheme for the town square of João Pessoa (fig. 23), a coastal city in the State of Paraíba. This was followed the next year by his design for the Ibirapuera Park in São Paulo (plates 50–52), a public project of enormous scale, intended to celebrate the four-hundredth anniversary of the founding of the city in 1954 and including buildings by Niemeyer. Although the Burle Marx scheme was never realized, his plan was carefully resolved. The large area of monumental proportions was broken up with elevated walkways set at varying heights and angles (see plate 51), manipulating the visitor's perspective as he passed through a series of intimate garden vignettes. The plan also called for the use of both contemporary and traditional building materials—foils for a collection of richly colored and textured Brazilian plants—as well as mirrored pools of water for floating parterres and fountains deployed as "liquid sculpture." Throughout the project, according to Burle Marx, he experimented with new means of expressing concepts of landscape-gardening history, in a continuum of themes found in the alcázar gardens of Seville, the Villa d'Este in Tivoli, and the Boboli Garden in Florence. The link between the flora and the architecture was paramount, and no protopostmodern historicism was even hinted at. It is during this period that Burle Marx exercised resolute control over both plant material and design. Tropical exuberance was restrained and single plant families were deployed in minimal groupings. In the Ibirapuera Park plan, lines of Carib royal palms (*Roystonia oleraceae*) are placed in a sequence of flower beds along a stone or mosaic walk. The color, shape, and texture of different species of philodendron fill in the background. At João Pessoa, the design exploits the subtle contrasts between columns of palms and the changing colors of their trunks, "going from coffee brown to orange to lettuce green, at different times of the year."[27]

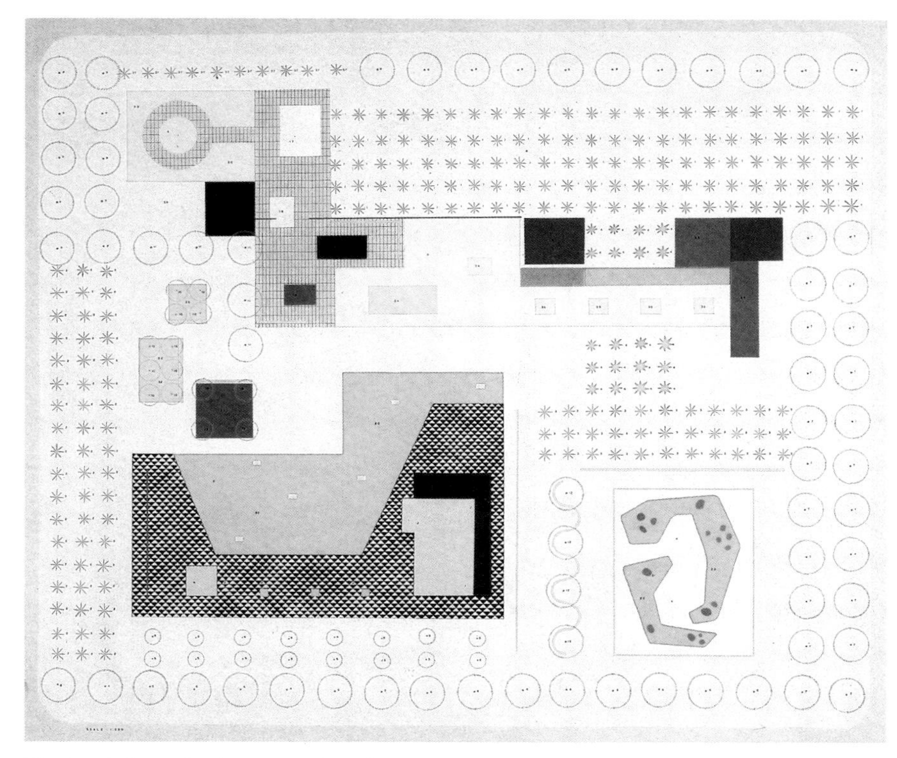

Fig. 23. Roberto Burle Marx. Plan of Praça da Independência (public square), João Pessoa, Paraíba, 1952. Gouache on board, 39 x 59 $^1/_2$ in. (100 x 151.2 cm)

Great colonnades of royal palms [are] *linked to other colonnades by means of a delicate avenue of Assai Euterpepalms (*Euterpe oleraceae*) and the sand-loving Macauba palm (*Acrocomia intumescens*), with its swollen trunk. Shade colonnades are created by the mass planting of* Pau darco; *and along the*

Fig. 24. Roberto Burle Marx. Garden of the Hospital Sul-America, Rio de Janeiro, 1955 (designed by architects Oscar Niemeyer and Helio Uchoa)

*sharply rectangular blue lake, lined with glass mosaic, the verticals perpendicular to it were created by the Aninga (*Montrichardia liminifera*), a spear-shaped plant, its reflection in the water giving it twice the height.*[28]

However abstract Burle Marx's garden designs may appear to be in his lyrical descriptions or in a photograph, they remain fundamentally concrete in what Le Corbusier called their "layers of organic equilibrium." These levels of harmony are evident in the small masterpiece created for the Hospital Sul-America, Rio de Janeiro, in 1955 (fig. 24), now destroyed. The garden's simple bench might have been lifted from an eighteenth-century *bosquet* designed for Versailles (fig. 25). The wall, lawn, and paved walks of the Burle Marx design are held together by an interior mathematics, suggesting, according to Flavio Motta, who knew the garden before it was destroyed, something as ancient as it is contemporary. In its control of proportion, the design introduces qualities of distinction and dignity that Le Corbusier called for when he spoke of the collaboration between architecture and art.[29] Here the transitory world of plants and the permanence of stone, concrete, and earth have been brought together by the artist with consummate skill and economy.

The sheer range in scale of Burle Marx's work over the years has been breathtaking, moving with ease from a small private garden that may be little more than a decorated wall of a few yards to a large creation such as the

Parque del Este, in Caracas, Venezuela, of 1956–61, a 175-acre public park that is now badly neglected. His versatility comes into even sharper focus if one compares his jewelry and textile designs made in his studio at Campo Grande and his plan for Flamengo Park (plates 53–55), a 289-acre park and parkway stretching along the coast in downtown Rio. If one considers that he also designed the nearly four-mile length of Copacabana Beach (plates 56–58), it becomes clear that Burle Marx has put his stamp on the entire central coastline of this unruly cityscape.

These grandiose landfills of the Rio de Janeiro waterfront over the last forty years were planned not only to handle the city's growing motor and air traffic but to provide space for new recreational and cultural facilities, setting them against the spectacular natural backdrop of bay, ocean, and distant mountains. The artificially created space also opened new prospects for the turbulent and increasingly ramshackle city threatened with isolation from its natural environment. The energy and technology required for this urban reclamation were monumental and demonstrate Burle Marx's repeated argument that our advanced means of destroying the environment in the late twentieth century can, with imagination, be used for the common good.

Architect Richard Neutra once said to Burle Marx: "I find no roots of the past in your art,"[30] ignoring all those transformations of history and antiquity carried out by Burle Marx in his own unique idiom, which has been filtered through a contemporary sensibility. At the Copacabana Beach of 1970 the waves of the Atlantic have been tamed and condensed into archaic patterns of black, white, and red mosaic, a series of abstract panels inspired by the the traditional mosaic pavements of Portugal known as *pedra portuguesa* and first introduced to the colony in the seventeenth century. By sheer bravado, Burle Marx acts as the arbiter in separating the entanglement of land and sea. Copacabana's roots actually reach back to the Roman colonies in Portugal of the second and third centuries A.D. Roberto knows the superb mosaic pavements excavated at Conimbriga (fig. 26), where

Fig. 25. Arbor with circular bench, Jardins des Versailles. Photograph by Eugène Atget, n.d.

Fig. 26. Central peristyle, House of the Fountains, Conimbriga, Portugal, third century. View of raised planting beds

Fig. 27. Roberto Burle Marx. Gardens of the Ministry of Foreign Affairs, Brasília, 1965. Detail of floating planting beds in water basin

the scale of the villa courtyard gardens had been broken up by a series of pools in which planted islands were placed in the water. These contoured beds emerging from the water in the center of a proconsul's peristyle garden suggested to Roberto a solution for unifying the water gardens surrounding the overscaled arcades of Niemeyer's Ministry of Foreign Affairs at Brasília in 1965 (fig. 27).

To see Burle Marx painting at Campo Grande, conceiving and organizing a new garden at his office in Rio, or closely observing the scientific characteristics of a species just rescued from an about-to-be-destroyed rain forest recalls a Renaissance *capo di bottega*, a master Florentine craftsman, in the words of his early biographer Pietro Bardi. He described Burle Marx as "clear-headed, simplifying problems and reducing them to elementary outlines, contemplating landscapes with the imagination of an artist and a whim for seeking out the unforeseen and occasional, uniting fertile reasoning to a knack for discovery."[31] It is all the more shocking, then, that Burle Marx was not encouraged to participate in the early planning stages of Brasília. He was not without critical supporters who shared his vision of "a tropical city . . . in the midst of plants, a city that is harmoniously thought out, systematized and built among trees, foliage, and flowers."[32] The lack of maintenance of the grounds and gardens he finally designed in the 1960s and the government's refusal to build his projected Botanical and Zoological Garden present a dispiriting picture. The essential harmony of architecture and landscape that is a vital element of modern Brazilian design genius is sadly missing. The scattered, surviving fragments of Burle Marx's work do little to humanize the intimidating and tattered spaces between the public buildings, shops, apartments, and hotels. By opening the hinterlands to man's progressive and relentless exploitation, Brasília is, in a way, a monument to the bankruptcy of the enlightenment's political and aesthetic ideals. In fulfilling the imperatives of economic development, letting the end justify the means in total disregard of the environment (a policy that has done so much damage throughout the world), the country proceeds at a relentless pace to lay waste to what is left of it.

Neglected and set apart, Burle Marx's enormous park in front of the Ministry of the Army, completed in 1970 (fig. 28; plates 59–62), strangely concentrates the alienated feeling one has in Brasília. In its isolation and surreal atmosphere, evoking the end of things, it would lend itself to a setting for a modern production of *Ajax* or *Oedipus Rex*. The biological vulnerability of gardens, and especially those with public ambitions, subjects them to this kind of romantic interpretation, but the ticking of nature's clock is acutely palpable here. Burle Marx's own tragic vision of the garden-landscape as an ideal too complex to be fully realized and maintained becomes evident as the public decay advances across the expanse of faded pavements, evoking the melancholy that engulfed Marcel Proust in the empty, neglected gardens of Versailles on a November day.

The artist's calculated intervention of native grasses and low groves of indigenous trees into this space, where the contours seem to fall into shallow, featureless valleys, may have unconsciously anticipated today's bureaucratic indifference and exhausted revenues. These have been his nemesis, particularly in large public projects, throughout his career. The central pool with its jagged pylons careening out of the water (plate 62), suggesting tank barriers to discourage terrorists, will no doubt survive the last general in the nearby headquarters of the Army. An alternative interpretation of the sculpture identifies the crystalline forms with the local rock discovered beneath the soil when excavations for the city first began.

The interior foyer of Brasília's National Theater has fared much better in its enclosed and protected space. Burle Marx the architect has responded to the structure of the building, incorporating the shadows of its steel, reinforced concrete, and glass into his organic composition. The natural and the artificial are in perfect pitch. The punctuating rhythm set up by volumes of dark-green philodendrons flows throughout, animating the minimalist space and offsetting the deadening effect of its sloping ceiling line.

Le Corbusier's romantic roof-garden reveries, in which the denizens of urban society have somehow regained a sense of their own humanity through a reawakened contact with nature, seem far removed from the dry, flat garden on the eighth floor of the Safra Bank in São Paulo of 1982 (plates 37, 38). Here there is no bay, mountainscape, or valley of Petropolis to call in. Rio's Sugarloaf Mountain, with its chic scarf of clouds, has been replaced by faceless commercial buildings engulfed in sulfurous smog and presiding over raucous traffic in the heart of a city that now numbers fifteen million people.

The design itself has been laid out and framed on the flat roof without the addition of soil (plate 39). Abstract contours have been literally transferred from the plan into this denatured universe by means of composition pebble in contrasting colors, laid down on the tarmac roof. Apparently solid, the stones are actually porous and absorb water. The garden is a tabula rasa that could only call forth illusions. The spiky potted plants would look at home on the moon, yet they enrich the hermetic system of this synthetic roof ecology, a twentieth-century version of a Zen monastery garden. The satellite TV disc on a neighboring rooftop might be a metamorphosed lotus blossom. Like the Zen garden of Ryoan-ji, the Safra roof garden is to be contemplated from one side, where the priests' veranda has been replaced by the hermetic dining room of the bank.

Fig. 28. Roberto Burle Marx. Gardens of the Ministry of the Army, Brasília, 1970

The hillside of the Fazenda Vargem Grande (plates 27–33), which in 1979 Burle Marx was asked to transform into a garden, had in the nineteenth century been the center of a coffee plantation, one of the most devastating environmental scourges Brazil has known. Through the interventions of Burle Marx, whose realization of the garden began in 1987, the poetic and scientific have coalesced, turning this wounded domain into an ecologically ideal setting for an incomparable botanical collection. The physical evidence of ancient, and for a time highly profitable, sins against nature—the scarred slopes (fig. 29), the channels bringing the water from peaks of the Serra da Bociana to the washing tanks, the long terraces used as drying yards for the coffee beans, the stone retaining walls—has all been left in place. But now by a new command the water is directed to a botanical role as it supplies the life blood to the rare water plants, assuming a mystical function of renewal by salvation as it spreads throughout the garden. Guided in its movement by the artist's imagination, the water fills the pools where it is held for a time and then released to spread its presence and perform the ritual of purification. This is not to suggest that the artist has written some kind of theological or mystical narrative recast as a modern garden. The problems of trying to read a modern garden design as a "text" in the way one might explicate the classical imagery of Stourhead or the Villa Lante are daunting at best. Such a scavenger hunt through the gardens of Burle Marx, steeped in the principles of abstract design, would be pointless.

Somehow the naive idealism of the modern movement—particularly its willingness to accept Rousseau's sentimental view of nature's innate goodness—never appealed to the critical, skeptical side of Burle Marx the scientist. Le Corbusier's vision of skyscrapers, housing developments, and suburban villas nestled in nature's unquestioning, Edenic embrace was not a part of the Brazilian's landscape philosophy. His first philosophical assumption was not to recreate a tamed jungle and call it a garden. Rather it calls for "the same attitude which reveals the conduct of neolithic man: to transform the natural topography in order to adjust it to human experience, individual, collective, utilitarian, and aesthetic."[33] He has seen clearly that the order imposed on nature by art was the only way to control its seething excesses. "Art is a ritualistic binding of the perpetual motion machine that is nature," Camille Paglia has written in her essay on art and nature. Nor is that order "necessarily just, kind or beautiful," she reminds us.[34]

Imposing aesthetic order on a scale demanded by the turbulent, spectacular, at times harsh and cruel environment of Brazil required an equally powerful, uncompromising vision. It also required organizing skills, political savvy, and a towering self-confidence, qualities that Burle Marx combined with those of the artist and scientist. These qualities and his eagerness to strike out and explore new territory immediately appealed to the circle of young Brazilian architects who in the 1930s were themselves beginning to question every aspect of their profession. They quickly saw the connection between Burle Marx's experiments with the vegetal kingdom as he developed his design repertoire and their own search for an independent expression in architecture appropriate to Brazil. It was his understanding of the vagaries of nature and of plants, as Michael Lancaster has pointed out, that removed the temptation so common to both artists and architects to see the garden as a static creation.[35] As a consummate plantsman, he understands and enjoys the constant changes of both seasons and growth cycles, but his is the role of maestro indulging in creative play and "ornamentation" (using that word in a musical sense), so long as the overall balance of the composition is not dislocated. His fusion of Latin, tropical, and European elements offers a new, alternative landscape that overflows with zest and inventive flair, a foil for the architects' own immutable creations. "The parallel between the achievement of Burle Marx and that of modern Brazilian architecture is so close," the architect Henrique Mindlin wrote, "that with due allowance for the difference in scope and scale, they can almost be described in the same terms: emotional spontaneity, striving for integration with the circumstances of land and climate and reassessment of the plastic language and of the means of expression, all under a growing intellectual discipline."[36]

This critical enthusiasm also reached an international audience. Architectural historian Sigfried Giedion, in commenting on contemporary trends in Brazilian architecture of the mid-1950s, focused on a crucial point when he asked how it was all to be "related to nature in the environment in which it is taking place, with its tropical growth one can almost feel bodily?"[37] His answer was that Brazil had produced a world-class landscape architect whose work catered first to the eye yet had substantial intellectual underpinnings. There were critics, however, who saw Burle Marx's designs merely "as beautiful paintings done with greenery and exotic plants." His designs did not sufficiently "protest a hostile architecture," said Italian architect Bruno Zevi, in an address to the International Federation of Landscape Architects in 1962, and he questioned whether it was even possible to apply the Burle Marx garden and park designs to large cityscapes. For others, the extent of Burle Marx's contribution was to produce a garden as a well-defined work of art, with little or no relationship to the surrounding landscape or urban environment. This criticism tended to ignore the brilliance of his responsive settings for the Odette Monteiro Garden in Correias of 1948 (plates 14–17), and for the Museu de Arte Moderno in Rio de Janeiro of 1954 (plate 54). It also ignored the obvious triumphs of the beachfronts and parkways in Rio, and overlooked the sheer variety and originality contained in perhaps the most extensive and still-growing body of landscape design in this century.

A critical reappraisal of garden and landscape design in the twentieth century has yet to be written. As Steven Krog has pointed out, the seeming absence of any reasoned ideas for the garden in our time has brought on a crisis of professional self-doubt that could be alleviated by placing in critical perspective the achievements of Burle Marx and other designers of his generation. So far, the record suggests, it has not been considered essential or relevant to do so. Yet the examination of even a small part of the work of Roberto Burle Marx reveals an artist of lasting stature and significance—one who is prepared to be taken seriously. His vision of nature is tragic and complex. And although he may never fully realize that vision, his work instructs us in its rich compendium of understanding distilled from a lifetime of experience, affections, attempts, mistakes, and successes.

Fig. 29. Roberto Burle Marx. Water channel of the original coffee-bean bath at Fazenda Vargem Grande, Areira, São Paulo

NOTES

1. Roberto Burle Marx, "Conceitos de Composição em Paisagismo," 1954; in *Arte e Paisagem: Conferencias Excolhidas* (São Paulo: Nobel, 1987), p. 11. Although excerpted in *Arte e Paisagem*, the complete manuscript in English translation has been made available to me by Denise Otis.
2. Joseph Rykwert, "Il giardino del futuro fra estetico e tecnologia," *Rassegna* (Bologna), no. 8 (October 1981), pp. 5–12; in English: "Aesthetics and Technology in the Garden of the Future," n.p.
3. The episode is described in *The Oxford Companion to Gardens*, edited by Patrick Goode and Michael Lancaster (New York: Oxford University Press, 1986), p. 409.
4. Steven Krog, "Whither the Garden," in *Landscape and Architecture*, edited by Stuart Wrede and William Howard Adams (New York: The Museum of Modern Art, forthcoming). According to Norman Newton, in *Design on the Land: The Development of Landscape Architecture* (Cambridge, Massachusetts: Belknap Press, 1971), p. 19, the first American course in landscape gardening was offered at Harvard University in 1900.
5. Norman Newton, "Modern Trends: What Are They?" *Landscape Architecture*, vol. 22, no. 4 (July 1932), p. 303; quoted in Krog, n.p.
6. Joseph M. Olbrich, "The Garden of Colors," 1905; reprinted in *Rassegna* (Bologna), no. 8 (October 1981), p. 13; from an address, "Der Farbengarten," delivered at a garden conference in Darmstadt, 1905, and published in Joseph Maria Olbrich, *Neue Gärten von Olbrich* (Berlin: Ernst Wasmuth, 1905).
7. Joseph August Lux, "The Garden Beautiful," 1909; reprinted in *Rassegna* (Bologna), no. 8 (October 1981), p. 15. Lux's statement first appeared in *Der Architekt* (Vienna), vol. 15 (1909), p. 120.
8. Richard Wesley, "Gabriel Guévrékian e il giardino cubista," *Rassegna* (Bologna), no. 8 (October 1981), p. 18; in English: "Gabriel Guévrékian and the Cubist Garden," n.p.
9. Roberto Burle Marx, quoted in Flavio L. Motta, *Roberto Burle Marx* (São Paulo: Nobel, 1984), p. 223.
10. From "Loudon, John Claudius," in *The Oxford Companion to Gardens*, p. 344. Burle Marx has frequently paid tribute to the English picturesque of the eighteenth century for its romantic influence on his work. While there is an inspirational link between the two, there is also an evolutionary connection with the crisp, asymmetrical French interpretation of the English gardenesque of the later half of the nineteenth century.
11. Alvar Aalto, quoted in Göran Schildt, *Alvar Aalto: The Decisive Years* (New York: Rizzoli International Publications, 1986), p. 221.
12. Roberto Burle Marx, "A Garden Style in Brazil to Meet Contemporary Needs," *Landscape Architecture*, vol. 44, no. 4 (July 1954), p. 202.
13. Louis Agassiz, quoted in Carlos E. Quintela, "An SOS for Brazil's Beleaguered Atlantic Forest," *Nature Conservancy Magazine* (Arlington, Virginia), March–April 1990, p. 17.
14. Elizabeth Cary Agassiz, quoted in Motta, p. 229.
15. Quoted in "The Architecture of Rino Levi," by Nestor Goulart Reis Filho, in *Rino Levi* (Milan: Edizioni di Comunità, 1974), p. 20.
16. Quoted in Pietro Maria Bardi, *The Tropical Gardens of Burle Marx* (New York: Reinhold Publishing Corporation, 1964), p. 12.
17. Camille Paglia, *Sexual Personae: Art and Decadence from Nefertiti to Emily Dickenson* (New Haven, Connecticut: Yale University Press, 1990), pp. 33–35. Paglia's essay "Sex and Violence in Nature and Art" discusses the fear of the eye in Judeo-Christian culture and accuses modern scholars of undervaluing the visual in their dependence on words and texts. She has touched on a pregnant idea worth considering in light of conventional architecture and landscape-design criticism. The garden is a sensual experience that begins with the eye, and this pagan quality has been repeatedly disguised or ignored by moralists throughout Western history. It would be difficult to imagine Burle Marx flourishing in a society less pagan, Latin, or sensual than Brazil's. The climate helps.
18. Harold Rosenberg, *Arshile Gorky: The Man, the Time, the Idea* (New York: Horizon Press, 1962), p. 32.
19. Quoted in Giuseppe Zambonini, "Process and Theme in the Work of Carlo Scarpa," *Perspecta* (New Haven, Connecticut), no. 20 (1983), p. 23.
20. Euclides Pimenta da Cunha (1855–1907) was an army officer, engineer, novelist, and journalist who brought to public attention the efforts of landless peasants in northeastern Brazil to found a self-supporting agricultural community called Comidos. Although the movement was finally suppressed by the army, it is considered one of the first to have attempted spontaneous democratic activity in Brazil. The motif of the Recife garden commemorating Euclides da Cunha recalls the desert that the community passed through in its search for independence.
21. Le Corbusier (Charles-Édouard Jeanneret), "La Rue," *L'Intransigéant* (Paris), May 1929; quoted in Pierre-Alain Croset, "Roof Gardens: The 'Technical Reason' and the Aesthetic Ideal," *Rassegna* (Bologna), no. 8 (October 1981), n.p.
22. Roberto Burle Marx, quoted in G. A. Jellicoe, "Scale, Diversity, and Space," *Studies in Landscape Design*, vol. 1 (London: Oxford University Press, 1960), p. 106.
23. Henrique E. Mindlin, *Modern Architecture in Brazil* (New York: Reinhold Publishing Corporation, 1956), p. 240.
24. *Ibid.*, p. 13.
25. Quoted in *Rino Levi*, p. 21.
26. *Ibid.*, p. 19.
27. Burle Marx, "A Garden Style in Brazil," p. 205.
28. *Ibid.*, p. 206.
29. Le Corbusier, "Architecture and the Arts," *Daedalus* (Cambridge, Massachusetts), no. 89 (1960), p. 49.
30. Quoted in Bardi, p. 12.
31. *Ibid.*, p. 16.
32. Roberto Burle Marx, "Arquitetura e arquitetura de Jardins," *Habitat* (São Paulo), no. 13 (December 1953), pp. 52–53. English summary.
33. Burle Marx, "Conceitos de Composição em Paisagismo," n.p.
34. Paglia, p. 29.
35. Michael Lancaster, "The Style of Burle Marx," *Hortus: A Garden Journal* (Wales), vol. 1 (Summer 1987), p. 46.
36. Mindlin, p. 13.
37. Sigfried Giedion, Preface to Mindlin, p. x.

Projects

EARLY DRAWINGS AND PROJECTS

Roberto Burle Marx was just nineteen years old when he traveled to Europe with his family in 1928. Settling in Berlin, where his father, Wilhelm Marx, had business, they remained in Germany eighteen months. During this time the young Burle Marx studied painting and voice and discovered the tropical plants of Brazil in the Dahlem Botanic Garden.

While in Berlin, Burle Marx developed the habit of sketching and made his first tentative plant drawings. In 1934, after completing his painting studies at the school of fine arts in Rio de Janeiro, he pursued his interest in plants and was named curator of parks in Recife, in northeastern Brazil, where he began to redesign the gardens of the city. His sketches during this period reveal his interest in both the character and structure of indigenous plants. From the beginning, he searched them out as a hunter, studying their personalities and habitats in minute detail, finding they engaged his mind as a scientist and his eye as a painter. "One may think of a plant as a brushstroke, as a single stitch of embroidery," he once said, "but one must never forget that it is an individual living plant." Several species of plants are named for him.

1

2

3

4

1. Study for a Garden, Berlin, 1929
Pastel on paper, 11 3/4 x 18 1/8 in. (30 x 46 cm)

2. Study for a Garden, 1937
Pastel on paper, 20 1/2 x 11 3/4 in. (52 x 30 cm)

3. Ten Studies for Tropical Gardens
Recife, Pernambuco, c. 1935–36
Ink on paper, 18 7/8 x 26 3/4 in. (48 x 68 cm)

4. Town Square, Recife, Pernambuco, 1935
Ink on paper, 16 1/8 x 25 1/4 in. (41 x 64 cm)

5

6

5. Gardens of Casa Forte
Recife, Pernambuco, 1935
India ink on paper, 19 1/4 x 25 1/8 in. (49 x 64 cm)

6. Gardens of Casa Forte
Recife, Pernambuco, 1935
India ink on paper, 16 7/8 x 22 in. (43 x 56 cm)

7. Praça do Entroncamento
Recife, Pernambuco, 1936
India ink on paper, 24 3/8 x 20 1/8 in. (62 x 51 cm)

8. Paláçio das Prinçesas
Recife, Pernambuco, 1936
India ink on paper, 18 1/8 x 23 1/4 in. (46 x 59 cm)

7

8

9

9. Praça Euclides da Cunha (*Cactário da Madalena*)
Recife, Pernambuco, 1935
Ink on paper, 15 3/4 x 20 1/2 in. (40 x 52 cm)

10. Flamboyant (*Delonix regia*)
Araruama, Rio de Janeiro, 1937
India ink on paper, 11 x 15 in. (28 x 38 cm)

11. Yacaré (*Pithecolobium tortum*), 1964
India ink on paper, 19 3/4 x 27 1/2 in. (50 x 70 cm)

10

11

PRIVATE GARDENS

Burle Marx received his first commission in 1932, when he designed a small roof garden for the Alfredo Schwartz House in Rio de Janeiro (see fig. 15). Since then he has created an extraordinary range of residential gardens, some of them intimate, idiosyncratic, and improvisational. Others are comparable in scale to the elaborate European creations of the eighteenth and nineteenth centuries.

Burton Tremaine Residence: Project

SANTA BARBARA, CALIFORNIA, 1948

Although Burle Marx is quite capable of challenging or ignoring indifferent architecture in his garden designs, he actively responded to the strong contrapuntal rhythms of the Burton Tremaine House, designed by Brazilian architect Oscar Niemeyer.

12

12. Model
Wood and cardboard
1 3/4 x 35 1/2 x 21 1/4 in. (4.5 x 90 x 54 cm)
The Museum of Modern Art, New York
Gift of Mr. and Mrs. Burton Tremaine

13. Garden plan
Gouache on paper
50 1/4 x 27 3/4 in. (127.7 x 70.5 cm)
The Museum of Modern Art, New York
Gift of Mr. and Mrs. Burton Tremaine

13

Odette Monteiro Estate

CORREIAS, RIO DE JANEIRO, 1948

In the dramatic scale, use of color, and plastic composition of the Odette Monteiro garden, adjacent to the house designed by architect Wladimir Alves de Souza, Burle Marx created one of his most influential designs. The tightly controlled lines of his roof gardens of the 1930s (see figs. 15, 19 and plates 34–39) are now recast in grand, baroque gestures, co-opting the mountains, forests, and sky and making the middle distance a part of the twentieth-century aesthetic. "For me," Burle Marx has said, "the constant interest of landscape gardening has been in reflecting the aesthetic feelings of my age in terms of plastic composition: space, shape, form, volume."

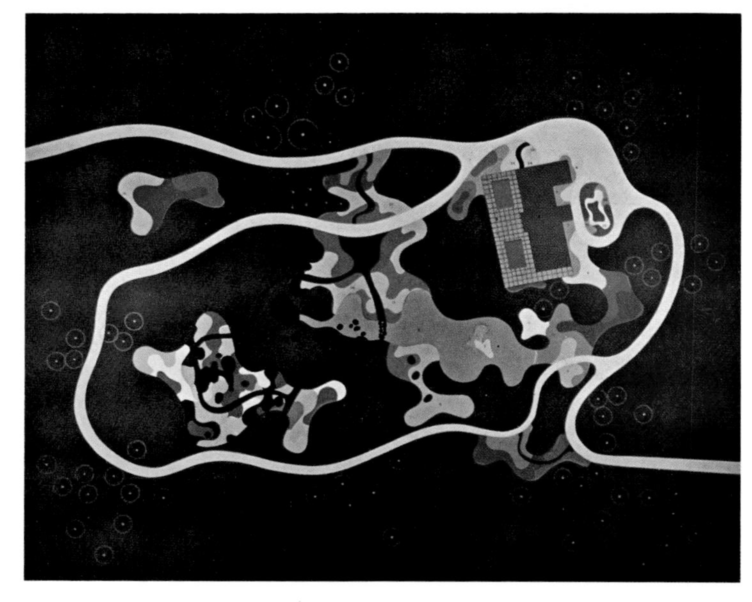

14

15

16

14. Garden plan
Gouache

15–17. Views of the Monteiro Garden, 1990

17

Olivo Gomes Estate

SÃO JOSÉ DOS CAMPOS, SÃO PAULO, 1950, 1965

The gardens of the Olivo Gomes Estate, which include a textile mill (Tecelagem Parahyba), and a residence, were created in two phases, the first coinciding with the completion of the house designed by architects Rino Levi and Roberto de Cerqueira César in 1950. Three years before, Burle Marx and Levi, traveling together in Europe, discussed the relationship between architecture and landscape design. According to Burle Marx, writing after Levi's death in 1972, they saw it as "beauty of form allied to function; interrelation of volumes, forms, and colors; aesthetics in relation to social and psychological ends." The results of this discussion are evident in their collaboration at São José dos Campos (see also Parahyba Dairies plant, 1965, fig. 22).

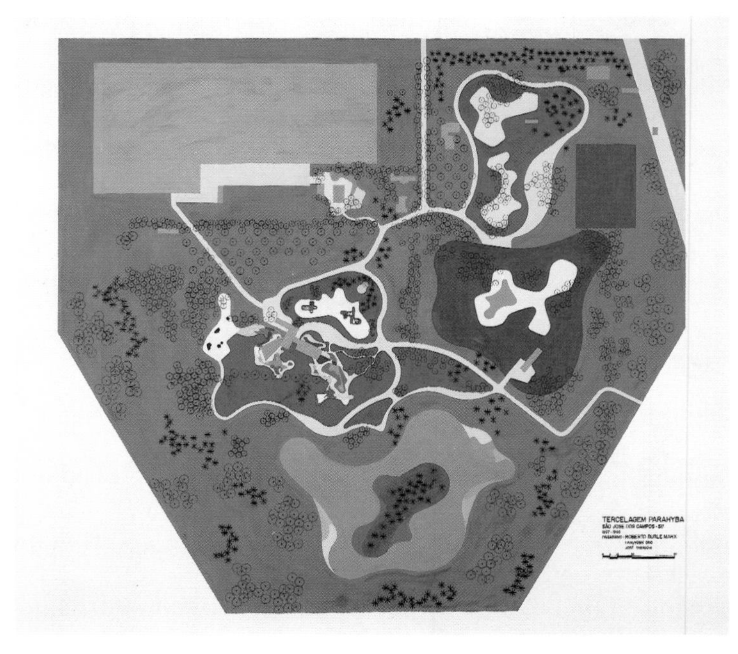

18

19

20

18. Garden plan, 1965 (redrawn 1990)
Gouache on paper, 38 x 44 1/4 in. (96.5 x 112.4 cm)

19, 20. Views of the lily pond and a row of Brazilian pine trees (*Araucaria angustifolia*), 1990

21. Outdoor theater in the children's garden of 1965, as viewed in 1990

22. View of the Olivo Gomes House and Garden, 1990

21

Mr. and Mrs. Gustavo Cisneros Residence

24

CARACAS, VENEZUELA, 1980

The garden commissioned by the Gustavo Cisneros family in 1980 for their residence by architect James W. Alcock follows by some twenty years a series of projects completed in Venezuela by Burle Marx. Between 1956 and 1961, while participating in the creation of the large-scale Parque del Este in Caracas, Burle Marx designed fourteen residential gardens in the area. It was at this time that he met Mrs. Cisneros, who admired his use of organic forms and the unusual spatial qualities he achieved. As in most of his gardens, water, plants, and light all play integral roles in the realization of his design.

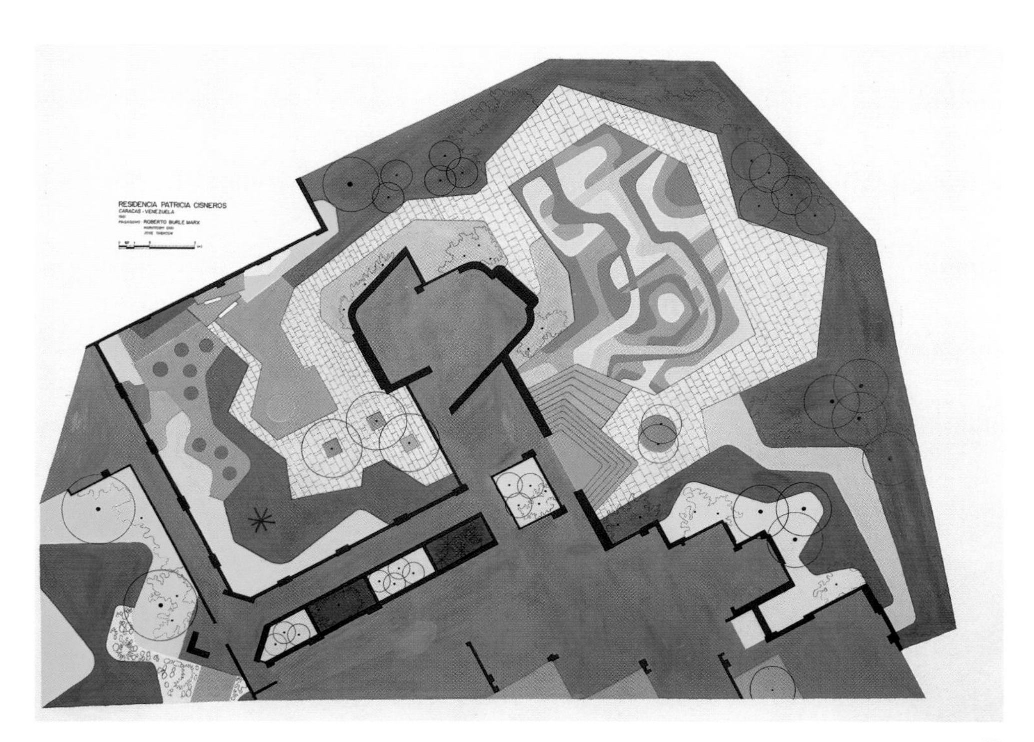

23

23. Garden plan (redrawn 1990)
Gouache on paper, 39 x 54 7/8 in. (99 x 139.5 cm)

24. View of the entryway, 1990

25. View of the pool with sculpted water race, 1990

26. View of the garden, 1990

25

26

Fazenda Vargem Grande

CLEMENTE GOMES ESTATE, AREIRA, SÃO PAULO, 1979–90

Work began on the garden at Fazenda Vargem Grande in 1987, although the plan was conceived in 1979. Despite the lapse in time, changes between the plan and the garden as it is executed are few. Many of its plants originated in Burle Marx's private collection at Sitio Santo Antonio da Bica (plates 44–49).

28

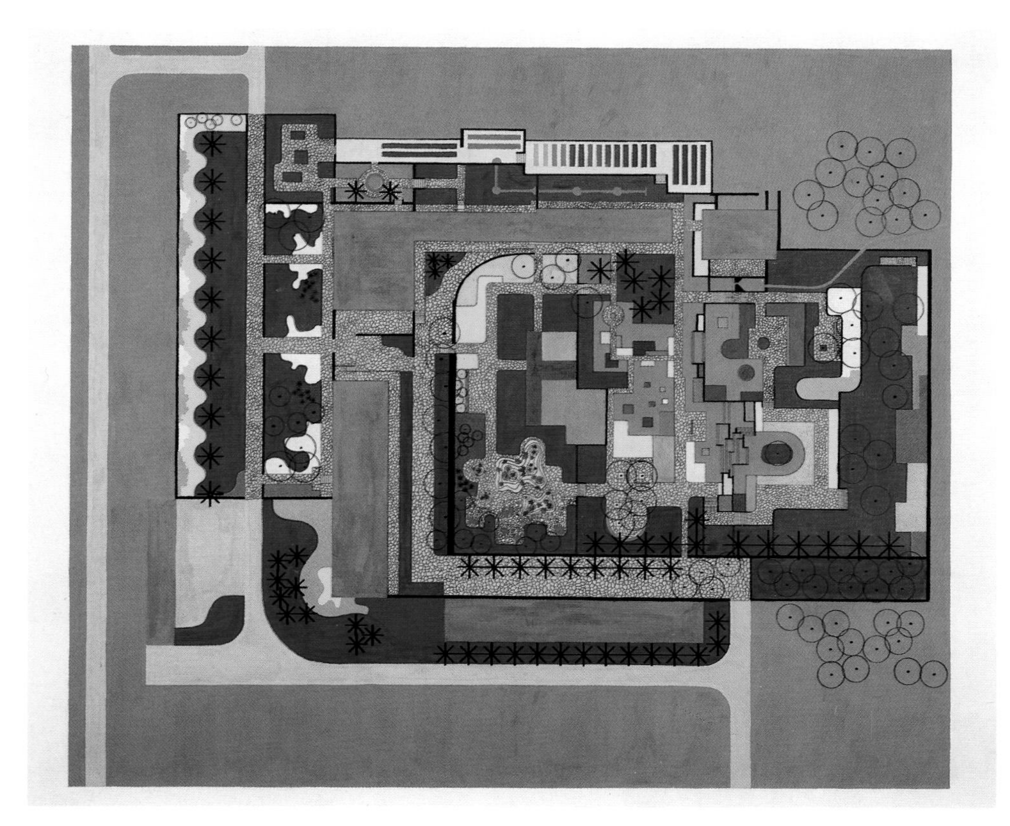

27

27. Garden plan, 1979 (redrawn 1990)
Gouache on paper, 38 1/4 x 45 7/8 in. (97 x 116.7 cm)

28. View of entrance to the garden, 1990

29, 30. Views of wet garden, 1990

29

30

31

32

33

31. Corner of dry garden, Fazenda Vargem Grande, combining stones and several varieties of plants

32. Rectilinear pool with Brazilian water-lilies (*Victoria regis*) in the foreground

33. View of wet garden with waterfall, 1990

GARDENS FOR THE WORKPLACE

"Form follows function" is a familiar dictum of the modern movement. Extending that philosophy into the designed landscape, Burle Marx addressed the vital garden possibilities of the workplace in the roof gardens of the Ministry of Education and Health, Rio de Janeiro, of 1936–38 and the Safra Bank, São Paulo, of 1982, as well as in his own working garden begun in 1949 at Santo Antonio da Bica, south of Rio de Janeiro.

Ministry of Education and Health

RIO DE JANEIRO, 1936–38

The Ministry building (see sketch, fig. 18), designed by architects Lucio Costa, Carlos Leão, Jorge Machado Moreira, Oscar Niemeyer, Affonso Eduardo Reidy, and Ernani Vasconcelos, with Le Corbusier as consultant, rises some eighteen stories above the two-story-high wing on which the roof garden rests. The Burle Marx design, part of the original scheme for the building, represents the artist's first experiment with organic forms, intended as much for the visual pleasure of the workers on the floors above as for the users of the garden itself.

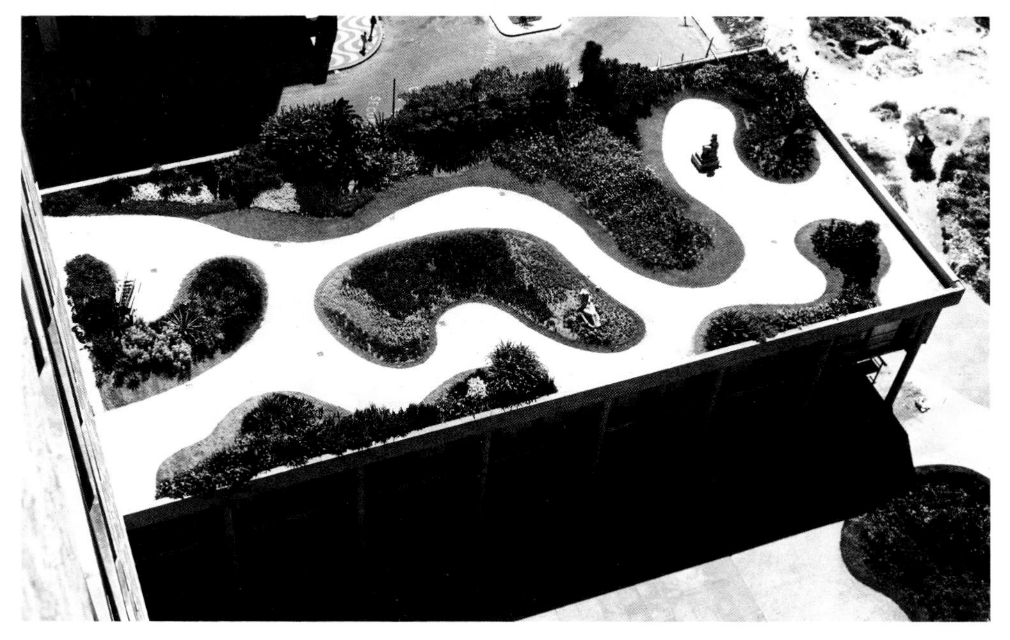

35

34

34. Plan of roof garden, 1938
Gouache on board, 39 x 59 1/2 in. (100 x 151.2 cm)

35. Roof garden viewed from an upper floor of the Ministry, c. 1945

36. Partially restored roof garden viewed from a nearby building, 1990

36

Safra Bank

RUA CONSOLAÇÃO, SÃO PAULO, 1982

Commissioned to create a roof garden adjacent to the executive dining room of the Safra Bank of São Paulo, Burle Marx returned to the organic lines of his earlier designs but executed them in artificial stone and potted plants. For a separate bank building, on Rua Bela Cintra (see pages 64–65), he created a wall garden and air plants set in moss panels, as well as an elaborate mosaic pavement design.

37

38

39

37, 38. Views of roof garden, 1990. Pebble-lined pathways suggesting a Japanese influence are punctuated by groups of Brazilian plants.

39. Aerial view of roof garden, c. 1982

Safra Bank

RUA BELA CINTRA, SÃO PAULO, 1982

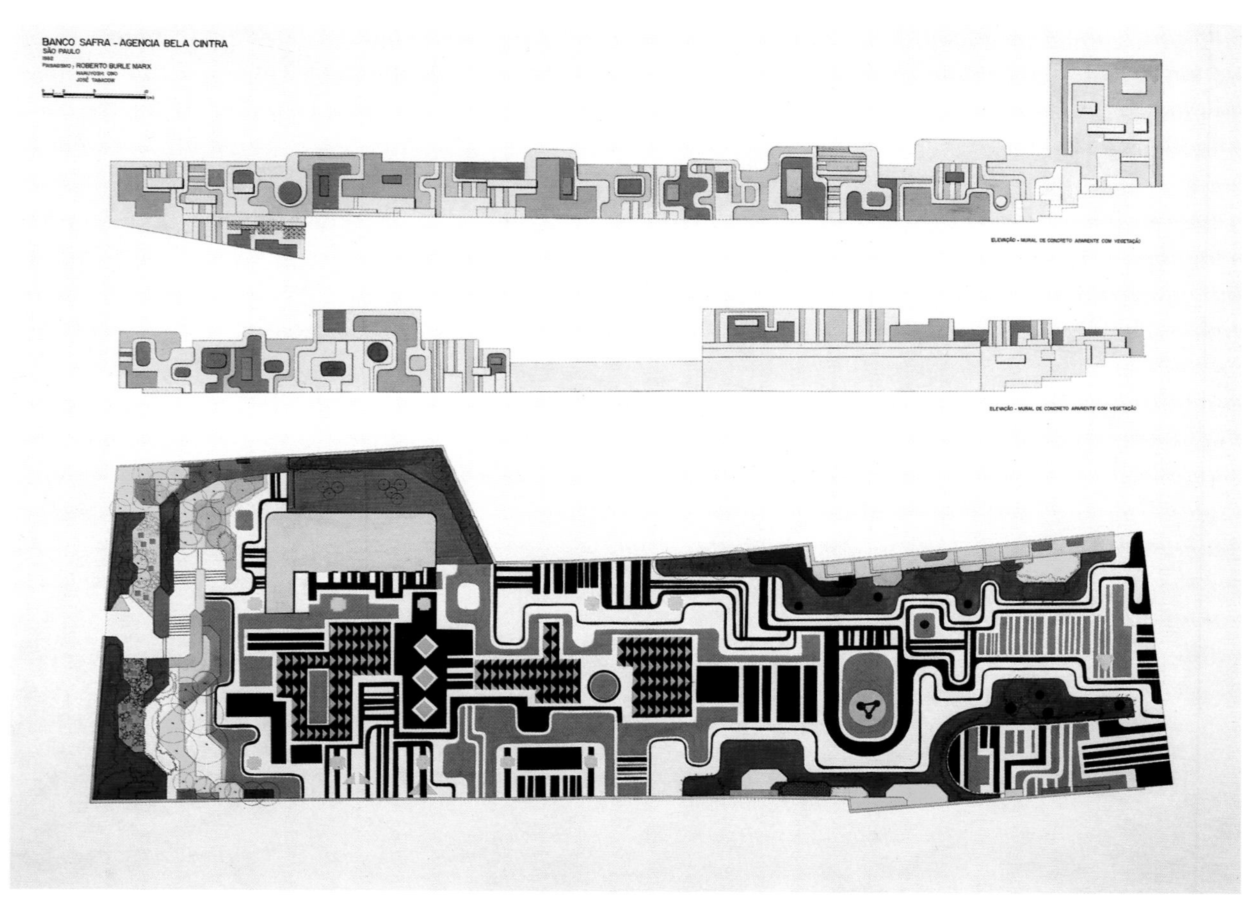

40

40. Elevations and plan of wall garden (redrawn 1990)
Gouache on paper
38 1/8 x 54 1/2 in. (97 x 138 cm)

41, 43. Views of wall garden, 1990. The mosaic-tile sidewalks were also designed by Burle Marx

42. View of plaza from the entrance, 1990

42

41

43

Sitio Santo Antonio da Bica

CAMPO GRANDE, RIO DE JANEIRO, 1949

A former coffee plantation located south of the city of Rio de Janeiro, Santo Antonio da Bica was acquired by Burle Marx in 1949 and since then has served as his home, studio, garden laboratory, and creative center of his life. Forty years of thought, improvisation, and change are built into its gardens, which contain one of the most important collections of tropical plants in the world. Most of the species in the collection were gathered by Burle Marx on his plant-hunting expeditions throughout the country.

45

44

44. A giant philodendron greets the visitor entering the Burle Marx greenhouse

45. Ceramic murals by Burle Marx decorate the walls of his dining room

46. Architectural fragments recovered from Rio buildings are found throughout the gardens

47–49. Three plant species found at Santo Antonio da Bica

46

47

48

49

PUBLIC GARDENS

In number and scale alone, the public parks, civic centers, and landscaped roadways designed by Burle Marx and his office in Brazil rival the output of Frederick Law Olmsted in the United States. Although the Burle Marx design for the monumental Ibirapuera Park in São Paulo never materialized, the giant landfill project for Flamengo Park in Rio de Janeiro stretches over some four miles of waterfront and encompasses, among other public facilities, the Museu de Arte Moderno and its garden. He also designed gardens for the Ministry of the Army in Brasília, the country's new capital dedicated in 1961.

Ibirapuera Park: Project

SÃO PAULO, 1953

Designed with Oscar Niemeyer to celebrate the Fourth Centennial of the founding of São Paulo, the elaborate plan for Ibirapuera Park (plate 50), 400,000 square meters in area, links a series of smaller gardens, including one with elevated walkways (plate 51) and another with rectilinear pools containing cubic planting beds and mosaic floors in designs based on carpet patterns from Bahia (plate 52).

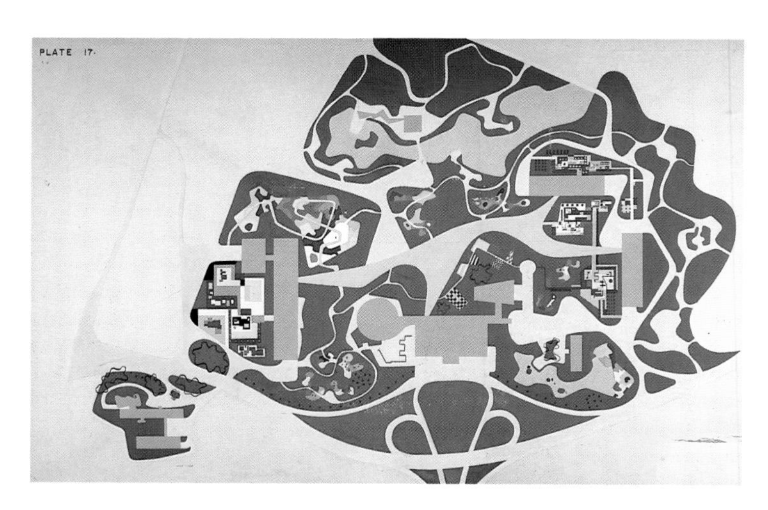

50

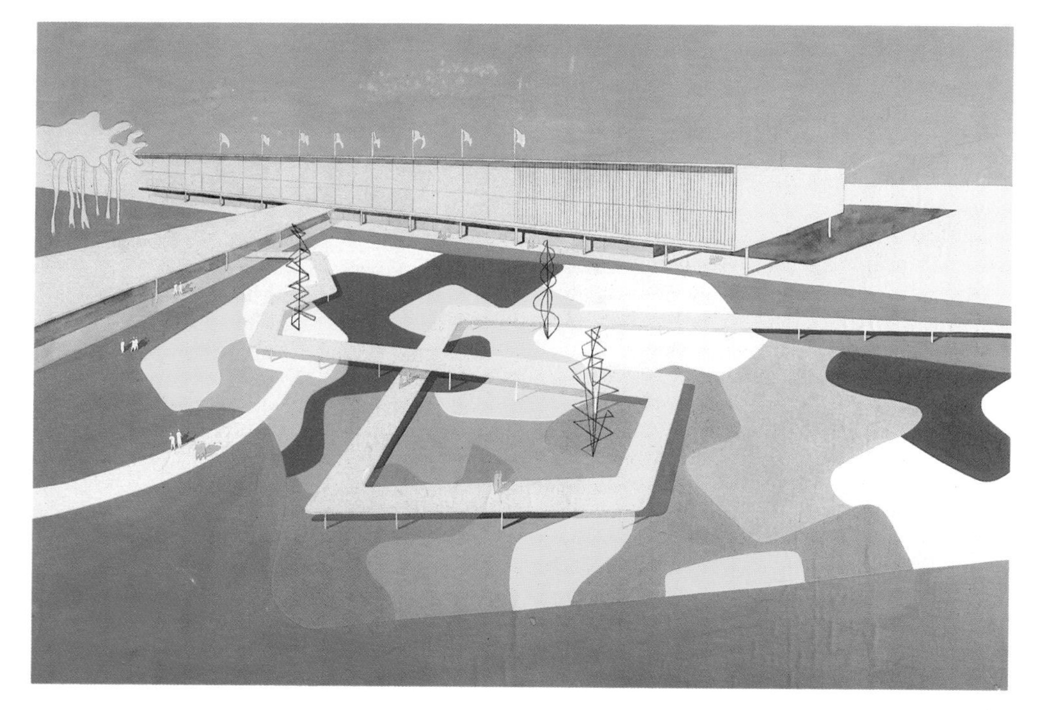

51

50. Plan (overall)
Gouache on board, 39 x 59 1/2 in. (100 x 151.2 cm)

51. Perspective rendering of Raised-Path Garden
Gouache on board, 39 x 59 1/2 in (100 x 151.2 cm)

52. Plan of Geometric Garden
Gouache on paper, 36 5/8 x 43 1/8 in. (93 x 109.5 cm)
The Museum of Modern Art, New York
Gift of Philip L. Goodwin

58

Bibliography

SELECTED WRITINGS BY ROBERTO BURLE MARX

"Conceitos de Composição em Paisagismo," 1954. Excerpted in *Arte e Paisagem: Conferencias Excolhidas*. São Paulo: Nobel, 1987.

"A Garden Style in Brazil to Meet Contemporary Needs," *Landscape Architecture* (Louisville), vol. 44, no. 4 (July 1954), p. 200–08.

"Giardini e Parchi presso Rio," *L'Architettura: Cronache e Storia* (Milan), vol. 10, no. 9 (January 1965), p. 620.

"Santiago Caracol: Headquarters of the United Nations Economic Commission for Latin America," *Progressive Architecture* (New York), vol. 47 (December 1966), pp. 158–59.

"An Exploration into the Use of Artificial Light in the Garden," n.d. English translation courtesy Denise Otis.

"Testimonial to Rino Levi," 1972. In *Rino Levi*. Milan: Edizioni di Comunità, 1974.

ARTICLES

Applegate, Judith. "Biennale 1970," *Art International* (Lugano), vol. 14, no. 7 (September 1970), pp. 82–85.

"Araxá, Brazil: Sulphur Springs Pavilion," *Architectural Forum* (New York), vol. 87 (November 1947), pp. 68–69.

Banham, Reyner. "The Profession of Landscape Architect and the Existence of Burle Marx," *Art News and Review* (London), vol. 116 (June 1956).

Bardi, Pietro Maria. "O Jardineiro Burle Marx," *Habitat* (São Paulo), no. 78 (July 1964), pp. 35, 41.

Best, Alastair. "Waste Land" [Exhibition: Royal College of Art, London], *The Architects' Journal* (London), vol. 175 (March 24, 1982), pp. 20–21.

Byrd, Warren T., and Susan S. Nelson. "On Drawing," *Landscape Architecture* (Louisville), vol. 75, no. 4 (July–August 1985), pp. 44–54.

Carelli, Emilie. "Roberto Burle Marx: Peintre du paysage," *L'Architecture d'aujourd'hui* (Paris), no. 262 (April 1989), pp. 92–95.

Carter, Allen. "Gardens: The Hidden Valley, Spectacular Setting in the Mountains above Rio," *Architectural Digest* (New York), vol. 37, no. 2 (March 1980), pp. 114–19.

Clark, H. F. "Reflections on Burle Marx," *Journal of the Institute of Landscape Architects* (London), vol. 38 (March 18, 1957), pp. 2–5.

Clay, Grady. "Brasília and Its Personalities," *Landscape Architecture* (Louisville), vol. 53, no. 4 (July 1963), p. 261.

Crease, David. Review [*Tropical Gardens of Burle Marx*, by P. M. Bardi], *Architectural Review* (London), vol. 136, no. 814 (December 1964), p. 397.

Dunnington Grubb, H. B. "Gardens of Roberto Burle Marx," *Royal Architectural Institute of Canada Journal* (Toronto), vol. 29, no. 2 (February 1952), pp. 42–44.

Eaton, Leonard K. "Landscape Architect Burle Marx: An Artist of Indisputable Significance," *Progressive Architecture* (New York), vol. 46 (November 1965), pp. 212–20.

Emanuel, Muriel. "Roberto Burle Marx," *Landscape Design*, no. 127 (August 1979), p. 15.

Giedion, Sigfried. "Burle Marx et le jardin contemporain," *L'Architecture d'aujourd'hui* (Boulogne-sur-Seine), nos. 42–43 (August 1952), pp. 11–14.

———. "Roberto Burle Marx und das Problem der Gartengestaltung," *Werk* (Bern), vol. 40 (August 1953), pp. 252–53.

Gómez Sicre, José. "Burle Marx of Brazil Designs Gardens for Today," *Américas* (Washington, D.C.), vol. 6 (July 1954), pp. 9–12.

Gregory, Frederick. "Roberto Burle Marx: The One-Man Extravaganza," *Landscape Architecture* (Louisville), vol. 71, no. 3 (May 1981), pp. 346–47.

Hamerman, Conrad. "Roberto Burle Marx: The Man and His Work," *Pacific Horticulture* (San Francisco), Winter 1985, pp. 22–30.

Hervé, Lucien. "Exposition Burle Marx au Musée Galliera, Paris," *L'Architecture d'aujourd'hui* (Boulogne-sur-Seine), no. 166 (March 1973), p. 116.

"Holiday Hostel at Tijuca, near Rio de Janeiro, for Employees of the King Insurance Company of Brazil: Views and Plans," *Architectural Review* (London), vol. 102 (December 1947), pp. 185–88.

"Jardins de l'aéroport de Rio: Vues et Plan," *L'Architecture d'aujourd'hui* (Boulogne-sur-Seine), no. 52 (January 1954), p. 33.

Kerner, Miguel Thomas. "Roberto Burle Marx: Parchi, giardini, ville, piazzi, spiagge," *L'Architettura: Cronache e Storia* (Milan), vol. 21, no. 12 (April 1976), pp. 716–30.

Korff, Alice Graeme. "Roberto Burle Marx of Brazil: Winner of the 1965 AIA Fine Arts Medal," *American Institute of Architects Journal* (Washington, D.C.), vol. 43 (May 1965), pp. 44–46.

Lancaster, Michael. Unpublished manuscript, n.d. Courtesy Denise Otis.

Lopez, Frank G. "Roberto Burle Marx: Art and the Landscape," *Architectural Record* (New York), vol. 116 (October 1954), pp. 145–151, 320, 324.

Marc, Olivier. "Jardins Brésiliens," *Aujourd'hui: Art et Architecture* (Boulogne-sur-Seine), vol. 8, no. 46 (July 1964), pp. 52–53.

"Miami Streetscape," *Landscape Architecture* (Louisville), vol. 79, no. 2 (March 1989), p. 16.

Motta, Flavio. "Four Gardens by Roberto Burle Marx," *Architectural Forum* (New York), vol. 87, no. 5 (November 1947), pp. 90–91.

"Musée d'art moderne à Rio de Janeiro: Les Jardins," *L'Architecture d'aujourd'hui* (Boulogne-sur-Seine), nos. 67–68 (October 1956), pp. 158–59.

"Neue Arbeiten des brasilianischen Gartengestalters im Kunstgewerbemuseum, Zurich," *Werk* (Bern), vol. 43 (December 1956), supplement p. 247.

"Os jardins de Burle Marx," *Habitat* (São Paulo), no. 3 (April–June 1951), pp. 7–15.

Otis, Denise. "Artist of the Garden: The Extraordinary Landscape Designs of Brazil's Roberto Burle Marx," *House and Garden* (New York), vol. 158, no. 9 (September 1986), pp. 166–77, 220–28.

"Pavilon du Brésil à Bruxelles: Le Jardin," *L'Architecture d'aujourd'hui* (Boulogne-sur-Seine), no. 29 (June 1958), p. 32.

Playfair, Guy. "The Versatility of Burle Marx," *Architectural Review* (London), vol. 136 (November 1964), pp. 360–65.

"Project for House in Santa Barbara," *Arts and Architecture* (Los Angeles), vol. 66, no. 3 (March 1949), pp. 26–29.

"Report on Brazil: Gardens by Burle Marx," *Architectural Review* (London), vol. 116 (October 1954), pp. 244–45.

Review [*Tropical Gardens of Burle Marx*, by P. M. Bardi], *Werk* (Bern), vol. 52 (January 1965), supplement pp. 24–25.

Richardson, Tim. "Copacabana Pavements," *Architectural Review* (London), vol. 177, no. 1056 (February 1985), pp. 80–81.

"Rio de Janeiro Airport," *Architectural Review* (London), vol. 101, no. 603 (March 1947), pp. 83–88.

"Rio de Janeiro: Luxury Beach Hotel at Praia Vermelha," *Architectural Forum* (New York), vol. 87 (November 1947), pp. 74–75.

"Rio, Museu de Arte Moderna: Exposição Burle Marx," *Habitat* (São Paulo), no. 71 (January 1964), p. 102.

Rivera, William M. Review [*Four Artists of the Americas: Roberto Burle Marx, Alexander Calder, Amelia Peláez, Rufino Tamayo*, by J. Goméz Sicre], *Journal of Aesthetics and Art Criticism* (Baltimore), vol. 17, no. 3 (March 1959), p. 397.

"Roberto Burle Marx," *Habitat* (São Paulo), no. 71 (March 1963), p. 65.

"Roberto Burle Marx: Notes by the Artist," *Arts and Architecture* (Los Angeles), vol. 71, no. 7 (July 1954), pp. 18–19.

Rykwert, Joseph. "Il giardino del futuro fra estetico e tecnologia," *Rassegna* (Bologna), no. 8 (October 1981), pp. 5–12.

Saarinen, Aline B. "Brazilian Pioneer: Landscape Architecture of Burle Marx Represented in Washington Show," *The New York Times*, May 30, 1954.

"Spring House at Araxá, Brazil," *Architectural Review* (London), vol. 102, no. 611 (November 1947), pp. 171–72.

"Trois Jardins de R. Burle Marx: Illustrations," *L'Architecture d'aujourd'hui* (Boulogne-sur-Seine), no. 49 (October 1953), pp. 91, 93.

"Work of Burle Marx on Tour," *Interiors* (New York), vol. 114, no. 3 (October 1954), p. 16.

Vincent, Claude. "Modern Garden in Brazil," *Architectural Review* (London), vol. 101 (May 1947), pp. 165–72.

Walmsley, Anthony. "Burle Marx, South America: Appraisal of a Master Artist," *Landscape Architecture* (Louisville), vol. 53, no. 4 (July 1963), pp. 262–70.

Zevi, Bruno. "Des jardins aux bijoux modernes de Burle Marx," *Architecture, Formes, Fonction* (Lausanne), no. 8 (1961–62), pp. 68-69.

"Zevi vs. Brasília: Leading Questions to IFLA Congress," *Architectural Review* (London), vol. 133 (April 1963), p. 234.

BOOKS AND CATALOGS

Bardi, Pietro Maria. *The Tropical Gardens of Burle Marx*. New York: Reinhold Publishing Corporation, 1964.

Bayon, Damian. "Roberto Burle Marx." In *The Changing Shape of Latin American Architecture*. New York: John Wiley and Sons, 1977.

Eliovson, Sima. *The Gardens of Roberto Burle Marx*. Foreword by Roberto Burle Marx. Portland, Oregon: Timber Press, 1990.

Frampton, Kenneth. *Modern Architecture: A Critical History*. New York and Toronto: Oxford University Press, 1980.

Goode, Patrick, and Michael Lancaster, executive eds. "Burle Marx, Roberto," In *The Oxford Companion to Gardens*, Geoffrey Jellicoe and Susan Jellicoe, consulting eds. New York and London: Oxford University Press, 1986.

Goodwin, Philip. *Brazil Builds: Architecture New and Old, 1642–1942*. New York: The Museum of Modern Art, 1943.

Goulart Reis Filho, Nestor. "The Architecture of Rino Levi." In *Rino Levi*. Milan: Edizioni di Comunità, 1974. Studies the relationship between Burle Marx gardens and Levi architecture.

Hitchcock, Henry-Russell. *Latin American Architecture since 1945*. New York: The Museum of Modern Art, 1955.

Jellicoe, G[eoffrey] A. *Studies in Landscape Design*, vol. 1. London: Oxford University Press, 1960.

Kassler, Elizabeth B. *Modern Gardens and the Landscape*. New York: The Museum of Modern Art, 1964. Reprint: 1984.

Mindlin, Henrique. *Modern Architecture in Brazil*. New York: Reinhold Publishing Corporation, 1956.

Motta, Flavio. *Roberto Burle Marx e a nova visão da paisagem*. Photographs by Marcel Gautherot. São Paulo: Nobel, 1984.

Niemeyer, Oscar. Foreword. In *Art in Latin American Architecture*, by Paul Damaz. New York: Reinhold Publishing Corporation, 1963.

Paris, Musée Galliera. *Roberto Burle Marx*. Exhibition catalog, 1973.

São Paulo, V Bienal. *Roberto Burle Marx: Sala Especial*. Exhibition catalog, text by Bruno Zevi, 1959.

Venice, XXXV Biennale. *Catalogo da representaçao do Brasíl: Pinturas, projetas e fotografias de jardins de Roberto Burle Marx*. Exhibition catalog, 1970.

Washington, D.C., Pan American Union. *Architecture in Brazil: Roberto Burle Marx*. Exhibition catalog, May 1954.

———. *Four Artists of the Americas: Roberto Burle Marx, Alexander Calder, Amelia Peláez, Rufino Tamayo*. Exhibition catalog, text by José Gómez Sicre, 1957.

Trustees of The Museum of Modern Art